An American

Impressions of

Mabel W. Daniels

Alpha Editions

This edition published in 2024

ISBN : 9789366386591

Design and Setting By
Alpha Editions
www.alphaedis.com
Email - info@alphaedis.com

As per information held with us this book is in Public Domain.
This book is a reproduction of an important historical work. Alpha Editions uses the best technology to reproduce historical work in the same manner it was first published to preserve its original nature. Any marks or number seen are left intentionally to preserve its true form.

Contents

I	- 1 -
II	- 12 -
III	- 19 -
IV	- 29 -
V	- 42 -
VI	- 55 -
VII	- 65 -
VIII	- 72 -
IX	- 79 -
X	- 84 -
XI	- 89 -
XII	- 93 -

I

MUNICH, *September 15, 1902.*

Dear Cecilia:—

Here I am in my Mecca at last after a "calm sea and prosperous voyage." Would that you were with me to share my pleasures, and, yes, I am selfish enough to add, my troubles, too, for you have such a magical power of charming away the latter that they seem but trifling vexations. Then I should so enjoy watching your delicious blue eyes open wide at these Germans and their queer customs, and oh! how you would elevate the tip of your aristocratic nose at my box of a study, which, however, I consider the height of cosiness and comfort—from a German standpoint.

Lest by this last remark I've imperilled my reputation for patriotism, let me hasten to assure you that I am as far from adopting a foreign point of view in my contemplation of Man and the Universe as when we used to walk from college down to Harvard Square and "have out" the discussions kindled by our four o'clock lecture. It's only in the concrete things of life that I've been forced to abandon my Bostonian, and therefore, of course, unimpeachable standards. I have learned how unwise a thing it would be for me to say to a German landlady, "Show me an apartment with running water, steam heat, electric lights, and a porcelain bath-tub." The poor bewildered creature would give me over at once into the hands of the omnipotent *Polizei* on the ground of insanity. But perhaps, after all, the best way of explaining myself is to follow the injunction in your letter: "Begin at the beginning and tell me all about it."

Mütterchen and I arrived at Munich late in the evening, and went directly to a hotel near the station, where we slept soundly after our long trip. Early the next morning I set out to look for a permanent abode. On my list were a number of well-recommended *pensions*, and I chose, naturally, the nearest at hand. It was not so easy to find as I had at first thought, for a German street has a queer fashion of changing its name every few blocks, so I deemed it wisest to inquire the way of a passer-by. Frankly, I had rather prided myself on my knowledge of the language, fondly imagining that I should have no trouble in understanding it or in making myself intelligible. With that sublime assurance born only of ignorance, I approached an honest-faced workman, and in a charmingly idiomatic sentence inquired the shortest way to Barerstrasse. He stared at me hard for a moment, and then burst into a flood of harsh-sounding words, not one of which fell familiarly on my ear. I was puzzled for a moment, but, thinking I must have mistaken his nationality, I bowed my thanks and made my way to a policeman on the corner, who, by the bye, wears a gleaming helmet like those of the soldier chorus in "Faust." His answer was fully as incomprehensible as the other, and I realized suddenly, with an overwhelming sense of helplessness, that this strange-sounding tongue must be the Bavarian dialect, and to understand it would require a totally new vocabulary. My enthusiasm was distinctly dampened, but I bravely opened the Red Book, which I had hitherto scorned, and unfolding the map of Munich to its full extent, I laboriously studied the tangle of black and red lines for a quarter of an hour before I found the desired street.

To reach the *pension* took but a short time, and I was relieved to discover that the landlady spoke north German and a little English. She was a large, red-cheeked, breezy person, and I felt very much like a small boat in tow of a big ship, as I meekly followed at her heels, while she showed me her vacant rooms, accompanying her smiles, bows, and gesticulations with a torrent of volubility. Finally she ushered me into a stuffy room, over-crowded with furniture, which she proudly called the "salon," and pointing out as *pièce de résistance* a decrepit, yellow-keyed piano, announced that it was "for the use of the guests." But the change, dear Cecilia, when I, like the stage villain, disclosed my identity! The alluring smile melted in a trice; the persuasive tones disappeared for the sharp rasp of the up-to-date business woman. I learned that a music student was regarded as an incubus, and shunned accordingly. Practice hours must be limited from, perhaps, nine-thirty to twelve and from four to seven. The only possible room was up four flights. Did I use the loud pedal much? Did I play any "pieces" or only "five-finger exercises"?

I cannot tell you all the questions she hurled at me. Suffice it to say, I left, downcast and disheartened, only to meet practically the same experience at each *pension* in turn. If there were already a music student in possession, that was the signal for me instantly to withdraw. If there were none, I found the rooms so undesirable, or practice hours so limited, that to remain was impossible.

At length I chanced to encounter, returning from her mornings work at the Pinakothek, an art student whom I had met on the steamer, and she told me of a house where she thought there were no *Musikers* as yet. With an anxious heart I hurried up the narrow stairs, and interviewed the landlady, who proved to be a most genial creature. An hour later we had left the hotel and were ensconced as proud possessors of two adjoining rooms. The larger we use for a sleeping-room, and the smaller is dignified by the name of "salon." It is there that I am to work, and I have already succeeded in making it a little more homelike, by placing a screen to mitigate the depressing hideousness of the stove, and by setting out my photographs on desk and table. I have, too, tacked on the wall the Glee Club pictures and several snapshots which you took that memorable spring day in the Yard.

The *pension* itself is small. Indeed, the *Frau Baronin*—which is the title with which I am to address my landlady—tells me she seldom has more than ten guests in the house. She also says that most of her *pensionnaires* are German, for which we are grateful. I cannot understand why so many Americans come over here expecting to see something of the life and then establish themselves in one of those hotel-like boarding-houses where the majority of the inmates speak only the English tongue.

The view from our windows is charming, for Maximilians-Platz is one of the most attractive spots in the city. As I look down on the waving tops, and green lawns dotted with flowers, I forget that I am in the city at all. Leaning out on the ledge, with the warm breath of the wind on my forehead, the twittering of birds and the soft plash of the fountain in my ears, the temptation to revel in all sorts of Arcadian dreams would be fairly irresistible, were not this idyllic illusion suddenly put to flight by the prosaic rumble of passing trams, which straightway brings me down to the commonplace.

Really, I didn't introduce that fountain just to create a romantic description, though it does sound rather like a daily theme. The best part of it is it's real,—and the loveliest thing in München. You can read about it any day in the Red Book, and can discover countless pictures of it, but, believe me, nothing can give you an idea of its sound as one stands at a little distance. If I were to score it I should use the strings and a harp—the former divided and subdivided as in the prelude to Lohengrin; and then perhaps I'd add a clarinet to give the effect of the birds' call which mingles exquisitely with the plaintive music of the water.

Later.

My first appearance in German society was made last evening at seven-thirty. We were shown by Gretchen, our stout maid, into the dining-room,—a large room with a long table in the centre, about which a number of people were sitting. At one end was the Baron. He is very fat, very jovial, and very red of face. Precisely the same adjectives somewhat intensified might be applied to his wife, who sat opposite. When neither of them was talking, they were laughing in the most infectious fashion imaginable. Isn't it queer to picture the nobility of Europe as running boarding-houses? I rather fancied I might see some of its members riding by in magnificent carriages, with high-stepping horses and clashing chains. I had pictured them as lounging against the cushions of their coaches with an air of bored grandeur, while somewhere in the background shone a glint of ermine,—but behold! German aristocracy bursts upon me in my landlord and landlady.

Mütterchen was given the place of honor at the Baron's right. I sat next. My *vis-à-vis* was a Frenchman whom I heard them addressing as "Herr Doktor." He was as typical of his nation as the Baron of his, and surveyed me critically from behind his gold-rimmed spectacles. It did not take me long to discover that he was intensely proud of his English, which was very bad. On his left sat Frau von Waldfel, a Hungarian, who monopolized the conversation in a high, rasping voice, and whose red cheeks, prominent nose, and beady black eyes bespoke aggressiveness of the most aggressive type. Then came Karl, the Baron's son, a stout, mischievous, frank-faced boy of fourteen, and on my right hand sat a blond-haired young man of about five and twenty, whom I should have acknowledged handsome had not his face been disfigured by several scars. I put him down at once as a student, for I had not travelled through Heidelberg on my way southward without learning something of the duelling custom. We were eight in all.

The first meal in a strange *pension* is an awful ordeal. We both rather dreaded it, the more so as no one present spoke English, except Frau von Waldfel, and we were rather timid about airing our knowledge of German. Then, too, every one seemed to converse so fast that the words fairly tumbled over one another. Whenever I heard a totally strange phrase I soothed my pride by saying, *sotto voce*, to *Mütterchen*, "Again that demoniacal dialect!" The Baron and Baroness were extremely kind, however, and did their utmost to make us feel at home, while Frau von Waldfel was in her element. These foreigners do so appreciate an opportunity to practise their English!

Between the continual making and consuming of numberless small sandwiches, which she prepared in a marvellously skilful fashion from her bread and butter, she conversed in the following manner, never pausing for a reply:

"Have you been to Dresden or Hamburg or Berlin? I don't care for those cities at all. They're frightful. Why, they simply starve you! Of course in Hamburg one does find good meat pie; the only decent thing in Dresden is the pastry. But give me Vienna! That's the city of Europe! One can get most *be-au-ti-ful* things to eat there."

Shades of the Sistine! Fancy travelling through Europe "for thy stomach's sake"! Possibly, however, this is no more unworthy an object than that of an American girl whom I met yesterday. "Like Munich? I should rather say not. There isn't one decent shop in the place!"

Just to think of all the articles they are writing at home to prove that we are fast developing an artistic sense!

Anything more inconvenient than the arrangement of meals would be hard to find—with the exception of breakfast. This is served when and where you want it and consists of rolls and coffee. It seems we are especially lucky inasmuch as we receive honey also "without extra charge," as the Baroness impressively added. At eleven o'clock comes the *Zweites Frühstück* which I rather imagine I shall omit. At one occurs *Mittaggessen*, a pompous meal requiring at least an hour. At five every one has afternoon coffee and a bit of cake. I hear there are any number of beguiling outdoor cafés where one can sit under the trees and hear good music. At seven-thirty your true son of Germany hungers yet again, and *Abendessen* (supper) is served. If, however, one wishes to attend any form of entertainment he must eat a cold supper early, in a bare and deserted dining-room, for the opera and concerts generally begin at seven o'clock. Do not imagine, my dear, that the German can now go to bed satisfied, for the Baroness assures me that he either sets out at once for a beer-hall and lingers over his stein all the evening, or about ten he has brought to his room such soporific things as cheese sandwiches, cold sausage, and, of course, the inevitable beverage. It's simply impossible for people to be hungry here. They don't have time to acquire an appetite.

Good night to you now, for it is growing late. I wonder what it will all be like, everything seems so strange now, and I feel as though I were a year's journey from America. Well, I shall do my best to write you all that happens. My plan is to keep a musical journal; that is, a record of all that occurs relating to my studies, and occasionally you won't mind, will you, if I copy an item or two from that into your letters? It will seem so much more as though I were talking to you if I scribble down things from day to day and then send the whole off in a batch, instead of writing in the conventional way one generally does. There is a clock striking now. It must be that of the two-towered Frauenkirche which is so near. So this time really good night and *angenehme Ruh'*, which means "a pleasant rest to you!"

September 19.

It was with a certain repressed excitement that I made my way toward Ainmüllerstrasse, at half-past eight this morning, to pay my first visit to Professor Thuille. My letters of introduction were clasped tightly in my hand, and I walked so rapidly that by the time I found myself on the landing before his door, after climbing several flights of stairs,—you know every one lives in a *Wohnung* (apartment) here, and an elevator in a dwelling-house is an almost unheard-of luxury,—I was completely out of breath. It still lacked fifteen minutes of the appointed time, so I had ample opportunity to regain my composure as I sat in the cosy reception room into which the maid had ushered me. Behind the closed doors at the further end of the apartment I could hear a pupil playing a Beethoven sonata, and a man's voice occasionally interrupting. I adjusted my hat for the twentieth time, smoothed my hair back over my ears, and endeavored to appear outwardly as if I were not at all in a flutter of expectation. Perhaps my excitement was increased by the remembrance of the impression I had made at supper last night, when I casually mentioned that I had come to Munich to study composition with Professor Thuille. Every one became attentive immediately, and spoke in the highest terms of his genius as a composer. I felt not a little proud, and somewhat uneasy, at the thought of meeting him.

"Richard Strauss was a pupil of his," said Herr Doktor, calmly, as he helped himself to a third piece of black bread. Thereupon I really trembled. So now, in order to quiet my nerves, I began to look about me.

The first thing which caught my eye was a landscape in vivid blues and greens, framed in massive and evidently costly style. From the inscription beneath I gathered that this creation was the gift of a grateful chorus to their "beloved director, Ludwig Thuille." Over the bookcase hung several giant laurel wreaths, their leaves now crisply yellowing. To these were attached brilliant, silver-lettered ribbons which, as they floated flamboyantly against the subdued gray of the wall-paper, proclaimed that these tokens, too, were the gifts of appreciative souls. The table near the door held a beautifully carved loving-cup of silver also bearing an inscription. Truly, gratitude must be the virtue *par excellence* of Germany!

If I had insensibly acquired an impression of ostentation from all this array of tributes—a common custom of every artist here, they tell me—this vanished the moment the door opened, for Professor Thuille and anything like ostentation are as far from one another as the poles. I was surprised to see a man so young in appearance, for I had in some inexplicable way formed the idea that he was much older. My second thought was that I had never seen so charming and cordial a smile. Of course he shook hands, as all these people do, and bade me be seated while he opened the letters. He is short in stature, with sandy hair, and a long mustache curled up at the ends in true imperial manner. His eyes, blue and kindly, looked straight and sympathetically at me. His face is deeply lined and shows tense sensitiveness in every feature. The rather strained expression vanishes, however, the moment he smiles. As he turned over my letters I noted that the fingers of his right hand were stained a deep yellow; already the faint aroma of cigarette smoke had reached me. Intuitively I felt that these two things indicated one of his characteristics. I had happened on the *Leitmotif*, as it were, of Thuille.

"*Ach! dass ist sehr nett!*" (That is very nice!) he said, laying down the letters. "You know Herr Chadwick and I studied in the same class in the old Conservatory. It is indeed delightful to hear from him again. And now about yourself. I understand that you want to study composition with me, Fräulein," he continued, looking at me with kindly scrutiny.

"If you will take me for a pupil, Herr Professor," said I.

"I think we can arrange it," he said, smiling, "although my time is almost wholly occupied. Tell me what you have already studied."

Whereupon we launched into details, and he appointed next Wednesday as the time for my first lesson. He does not speak a word of English, and I found him exceedingly difficult to understand, but he assures me he is accustomed to foreigners.

"If we don't make ourselves intelligible," he ended, laughing, "we can try a few French phrases, or even a bit of Latin, as a pupil of mine did the other day." Instead of my taking leave of him there, he went out to the very door with me, which he opened, bowing smilingly, and as it closed I felt wonderfully less like a stranger in a strange land.

At the corner I took a tram back to town. They are all alike, very short, and painted the Bavarian blue. Think of a city so patriotic that the street cars assume the national hue! The conductor politely touched his hat to me as I entered. I thought he must have mistaken me for some one else till I saw him salute each passenger in the same courteous manner. Where Brienner-strasse meets Odeons-Platz I alighted. This is just by the Feldernhalle. If you have seen pictures of the Loggia at Florence you can tell how it looks, for it is a copy of the Italian building. Here I was to meet Fräulein L———. She is a friend of the Baroness and had offered to help me in hiring a piano. That elocution course of ours proved very valuable to me at this stage, for had it not been for the telling and effective gestures with which I supplemented my German I might have had in my study a far less acceptable instrument than the excellent Blüthner which now stands here and for which I pay the absurdly small sum of ten marks (two dollars and a half) a month.

"By the bye," said I, as we were walking through Theatiner-strasse, "did I make a great many mistakes in my note to you?"

I meant this to sound naïvely humble, but in reality I had spent a half-hour on the composition of those ten lines and I was rather proud of the result.

"Oh, no," she replied, smiling, "you merely asked me to meet you *on top* of the Feldernhalle. I was wondering," she added, mischievously, glancing as we passed at the building's imposing height, "just how I could get up there."

For several blocks I was silent, meditating on the sad results of "pride, rank pride and haughtiness of soul," although I fully appreciated her effort at a joke. Such pleasantries are almost unheard of in German girls, and whenever they do say anything facetious they look very much frightened, as though at a loss whether to apologize at once or explain how it came to happen. I must send you one of the comic papers. They considerately print the point of a joke in italics. One has at least the satisfaction of knowing when to laugh, a virtue not to be despised when one considers the subtleties of modern wit, so called.

"This is where I buy my music," said Fräulein L——, stopping before a small store, "and if it pleases you I will introduce you here."

Accordingly we went in, and after meeting the proprietor I was initiated into the mysteries of that very important factor in a student's life, an *abonnement*. One pays a small sum for the privilege of taking out music from a circulating library for a definite length of time. The arrangement impressed me at once as advantageous, and I inquired as to the kinds of music the catalogue contained. "Why, songs, operas, overtures, anything you care for," said the proprietor, in a patronizing tone.

"Then I can get orchestral scores," I said.

"Orchestral scores?" he cried, starting back as though I had asked him to pluck the moon out of the sky. "My dear young lady, what can you possibly want of orchestral scores?" We should call this impudence in America, but I really do not think he intended it as such. He had simply not come much in contact with the modern American girl. After explanation on both sides, I found, however, that it would be better for me to obtain scores from the Conservatory, which I intend to enter, and where, I learn, all the standard scores are on hand.

You would hardly believe me if I should tell you how many bareheaded, blue-aproned girls we met carrying beer through the streets during our walk home. But my surprise at the sight was lost in greater amazement at beholding the number of steins they are able to carry at one time. Not two or three, my dear, but six, yes, even ten, in one hand. It is an art in itself. If one is careless and holds the handful a quarter of an inch from perpendicular, the beer comes oozing out at the top and trickles on the sidewalk. This disturbs no one in the least. As we passed the droschky stand on Max-Joseph-Platz about eleven o'clock, there stood all the cabbies lounging against their carriages or ranged along the curbstones, leisurely drinking great steins of frothy beer which one of these blue-aproned girls had just brought. When they finished they set their empty mugs on the window ledges of the building. Imagine a dozen of our hackmen draining steins on Brimstone Corner and then leaving them in a row on the steps of Park Street Church!

How can I write you about the evening or rather afternoon and evening which followed? When I tell you that it was my first hearing of "Tristan and Isolde" in the wonderful new Prince Regent Theatre, are you surprised that I hesitate? I will let you read for yourself in the infallible Red Book of the unique construction of the house which is used for the reproduction of

Wagner's operas alone, of the peculiar stage, and of that stroke of genius, the concealed orchestra. If I attempted any explanations I should fail lamentably, for all else is forgotten in the memory of that glorious music. The crowd of magnificently dressed people promenading between the acts through restaurant, garden, and corridors, the strange types of musicians from every quarter of the globe, the trumpet calls to summon us back to our places—all are now a confused medley of impressions. I only see Knote, as Tristan, quaffing the fatal draught, and Ternina, a regal Isolde, waving her white scarf in the mysterious moonlight of that most alluring of gardens.

Who was it said that in Tristan the "thrills relieve one another in squads"? It seems to me there is no respite: one is swept along and borne aloft uninterruptedly by the power of the music—music magical in its chromatic beauty, tremendous in its intensity. Breathless, at the final fall of the curtain, I hardly realized my physical exhaustion till we reached home. The strain in endeavoring to follow the multi-woven orchestration, as well as the action, had not been a light one.

During one of the pauses I caught sight of a slender, rather pale young man elbowing his way through the crowd. I turned to look at him, for his face struck me as strangely familiar. Who do you think it was? *Siegfried Wagner!* Fancy what his feelings must be to see all this homage paid to his father's genius.

Sunday.

As a result of my intoxication last night—if one may so call it—I overslept this morning and was in danger of being late to church. In fact, the people were already on their knees when we entered the little chapel which is the home of American church life here. The name chapel is only applied out of compliment, for it is really a large room with improvised altar at one end, a piano in the corner, and rows of chairs for pews. It seemed, however, as fine as a cathedral to us, and how beautiful it sounded to hear those familiar old prayers again in our mother tongue, while everywhere without these walls was the babble of a foreign language.

At the close of the service, as the rector was reading that most impressive of prayers, the prayer for those at sea, and we were following with more than usual devoutness, for the dangers and perils of the great deep were still very real to us, bang! the blare of trumpet, thud of drum, and thunder of trombone burst on the stillness, and the sound of a lively march, the sort to make one's feet tingle, came ever louder and louder to our ears. I expected to see the rectors face change and to hear him hurriedly close, but no, his voice kept on peacefully, unconcernedly, and the people knelt absorbed as though the thought of worldly things was far removed. I must confess I found it hard to keep my mind fastened on the spiritual; it was my first experience of hearing anything from the ritual accompanied by Sousa music, and the irreverence shocked me.

I was eager to inquire about the music, but after the service, as we reached the end of the aisle, the rector came forward with outstretched hand. The consul, to whom we had letters, had told him of the two new strangers in the colony, and his welcome was most cordial.

"I want you both to come to tea at the Russicher Hof to-morrow, if you will pardon the unconventionally of my invitation," said his wife, a bustling little woman in black. "There will be several music students on hand and it may be pleasant for you to meet one another." We thanked her heartily. One appreciates these things so much when away from home.

The music had now begun again, this time abandoning the martial for the romantic, and giving out the opening strains of Von Weber's overture to *Der Freischütz*.

"It's more than a brass band," said I, urging *Mütterchen* along. "There are clarinets and flutes. Do let's hurry."

We turned down the little archway which led from the chapel door to the main street, and *voilà!* there was a picture well worth seeing. Have I explained that in front of the Feldernhalle is a triangular open space? This now was thronged with a gayly attired crowd, who were promenading up and down or chatting in small groups, while from the balcony of the Feldernhalle itself came the sound of inspiring music played by the great military band of the city.

One caught the irresistible charm of color enhanced by sunshine. The scarlet uniforms of the officers who were everywhere, the bright caps of the students, the gleaming helmets of the officials set off against the dark background of the Alte Residenz lent an artistic touch to a scene already brilliant.

"Isn't it splendid?" cried I, excitedly, as we moved along with the laughing throng. "Just see, *Mütterchen*, there's an officer kissing that lady's hand. It's like a scene from a play."

"It's all a rather strange sight on Sunday," replied *Mütterchen*, smiling gently.

I suddenly remembered my Puritan ancestors and felt I ought to shut my ears to the fascinating lilt of the "Merry Wives of Windsor" overture.

"I don't believe Cotton Mather himself would call these people wicked," I said, with a glance at the happy crowd about me.

Just then the student from our *pension* passed us with a low bow. There were a number of young men with him, all wearing round caps of black and purple.

(The colors indicate the corps or club to which they belong.) Do you know that the men bow first in this country? To the masculine sex is allotted the right to accept or reject an acquaintance. Isn't that truly German?

We were glad that Herr Martens had condescended to recognize us, for it gave us a pleasant sensation to realize we were not utterly unacquainted in that great throng of people. Not two minutes later, who should swoop down upon us but Frau von Waldfel. Cecilia *mia*, don't let me hear of your banishing "swoop" to the category of slang. I am much attached to that invaluable word. Have you ever seen a gull circling with wide-spread wings above a fish in the water beneath, and then suddenly dart down and bear away his prey? When certain people accost me this picture invariably comes to my mind. Frau von Waldfel swoops down and captures one like the gull, while I play the part of the unfortunate fish.

"So you are enjoying the Parada, are you?" she began. She had once spent a season in London, and so caught the English habit of making her remarks interrogative. "We always have this music every Sunday. I've been doing a little shopping, you see, on my way home from church." (She pointed to a number of small packages under her arm.) "I've ordered some cakes sent up to the *pension*. Did you know the tarts here are not nearly so good as those in Berlin? Dear me, I have quite forgotten whether you said you had been there or not. Your daughter is such a quiet girl," she added to *Mütterchen*, "I never can draw her out."

Mütterchen gave an involuntary gasp at this last remark.

"Are all the stores open Sunday?" I said, endeavoring to show I could make conversation. All I needed was an opportunity.

"Of course! Why not?" she answered, as we turned our steps towards Maximilian-Platz. "They close at one o'clock; on other days at half-past seven in the evening. I'm a regular guide-book, much more practical than that red one I see you carry. Speaking of Berlin tarts, I want to tell you that I never ate——" and so on—can't you hear her?—till we reached the door.

We spent a quiet afternoon reading and writing letters. After supper the Baroness invited us to come into the salon. "I always try to make Sunday evening a pleasant time," she said. What was our surprise on entering to see them all seated around a table playing cards. They seemed much disappointed that we did not join them.

If this letter of mine is posted to-night, it will catch the New York mail steamer, so I shall send it out now by Georg, the man-servant of the house. *Auf Wiedersehen*, and don't forget I am hungry for news of everything at home.

II

October 4.

Top o' the morning, Cecy dear!

Such a glorious, *allegro vivace* day! The sun is shining, the air is crisp and cool, and the sauciest of breezes is coquetting with the tree-tops in the Platz. It gets into one's blood, a morning like this, and the wildest dreams seem possible of fulfilment. I came home from my lesson humming the theme of the scherzo of Beethoven's eighth symphony. It seemed to fit the buoyancy of my mood as nothing else could.

I can see you smile now and hear you say, "It's quite evident she is happy in her new surroundings." Exactly so, my dear, and there are so many delightful things to tell you about that I don't know where to begin. However, the Conservatory forms one of the most vital elements of my new life here, so I'll start by telling you of my first visit there.

Be it known, then, that the Royal Conservatory of Munich, to give it its full title, opened the eighteenth, and promptly at nine o'clock I made my way thither. What a rambling old building it is, and how replete with association! So many musicians have studied here at some time or other, although Rheinberger and many of the teachers who have made it famous are now memories of the past. With a certain indefinable thrill I realized I was actually within these walls.

Instead of the *Herein!* which I expected to hear in response to my knock on the door of the director's room, Stavenhagen himself opened the door. I wonder if you heard him play when he was in America. He's a handsome man, not much above thirty, with blue eyes, firm chin, straight nose, and curly blond hair and mustache.

In fact, he has all the delightful characteristics of a German, and none of the unlovely ones. Besides this, he is tall, a rarity in men of his nation.

"*Eine Amerikanerin!*" he said pleasantly, pushing a chair forward. "I speak a lee-tle English, but," he went on in German, "perhaps we will make more progress if I stick to my mother tongue."

"I speak a very little German," said I, smiling, not feeling in the least afraid of him, and forthwith explained my situation and what I wished to do at the school. A little man, whose face, beard, and hair all seemed the same reddish color, was looking over a pile of letters in the corner of the room. He now glanced up at me curiously as I began my inquiries about the *Partitur Lesen* (score reading) class of which I had read in the catalogue.

You know that five years ago women were not allowed to study counterpoint at the Conservatory. In fact, anything more advanced than elementary harmony was debarred. The ability of the feminine intellect to comprehend the intricacies of a *stretto*, or cope with double counterpoint in the tenth, if not openly denied, was severely questioned. This carefully nourished conservatism has yielded considerably. The counterpoint class is now open to women, although as yet comparatively few avail themselves of the opportunity. Formerly, too, all the teachers in the Conservatory were men, but one finds to-day two women enrolled as professors among the forty on the list.

"I should like to enter the *Partitur Lesen* class," said I, innocently, not then having learned all this.

Stavenhagen looked at the little man. The little man looked back at Stavenhagen. If I had thrown a bombshell they could not have appeared more startled. The little man at once abandoned his letters and stood staring, a few feet in front of me.

"There have never been any women in the class. I am right, am I not, *Herr Sekretariat?*" said Stavenhagen.

"You are right, *Herr Direktor*," responded the other. He held his hands behind him and gazed at me as one might at a curious species of animal. I felt I ought to be tagged, like those poor creatures in the Zoo, "Rare. From North America."

"Is the class full, *Herr Sekretariat?*" inquired Stavenhagen.

"About thirty men have registered, *Herr Direktor*," solemnly answered the secretary.

There was a pause.

"Have you ever played string quarters from score, Fräulein?" inquired the director.

"Yes, *Herr Direktor*," said I, with that supreme calmness which comes at times when one is inwardly much disturbed. Again there was a pause. Even I began to be impressed by the solemnity of the occasion.

"Of course," said the director, "because a Fräulein never has joined the class is no reason why a Fräulein never can."

"Not at all," said the secretary. The gravity of his expression was worthy a crisis in the affairs of state.

The two men walked to the other side of the room, and while they conversed in whispers I stood gazing out of the window at the equestrian statue in the

Platz, unable to hide the smile at the corners of my mouth. Although conscious of my many peculiarities, I had never before considered myself an abnormal being, and to be so regarded struck me as amusing.

It seemed to take them a long time to come to a decision. When my impatience had subsided to a state of hopelessness, Stavenhagen came forward.

"Your request is unusual, Fräulein," he began, "but—but—well, you may come on Friday at three o'clock."

With a sigh of relief I bowed myself out in approved German fashion, feeling as might the immortal Napoleon after a hard-won victory.

The first Kaim-Saal concert of the season came in the evening. The Kaim-Saal is a splendid hall with a large organ, where most of the concerts are held. There was a fine program including Beethoven's first symphony. I was greatly interested to see Weingartner conduct. He looked very young as he stepped to the platform. He is slight and dark, with brown, clever eyes. I must confess that at first I did not like his conducting at all. It seemed to me extreme and even sensational. However, as I became accustomed to his extravagant methods, the earnestness and power of the man impressed me more and more. When it came to the Beethoven number he directed without score. He fairly swept the orchestra along, and his every gesture was pregnant with meaning. I could not help thinking of Gericke's straight immovable figure as I saw Weingartner wave wildly to right and left, rise on tiptoe, sway forward, and now, by one tense, quick movement of his stick, bring his men to a grand climax. Sometimes he even let his beat cease entirely and his arm drop to his side, while the orchestra seemed to carry itself along like a wheel which continues revolving after the force which propelled it has stopped.

My enthusiasm caught fire from his, and at the close of the concert I was cheering as wildly as the rest of the audience. I can't tell you how many times he came forward to bow his thanks amid the cries of "Bravo! Bravo!" He seemed to enjoy it all hugely and kept smiling down on us. When he does that his face loses every bit of dignity and he looks like nothing so much as a roguish boy.

On our way down to the *Garderobe*, where every one checks one's things for the fee of twenty pfennigs (five cents), we met Mr. B——. He is a harmless young curate from the north of England; one of those men who have soft, gentle voices, Van Dyke beards, and always sit on the edge of a chair. He had been to the church tea that afternoon, and shown a praiseworthy desire to make himself agreeable.

"Ah, good evening," he said, "was it not a beautiful concert? And so uplifting! I see you have the score to—to——"

"The Beethoven symphony," I replied.

"Oh, yes. Beethoven has indeed caught the spiritual note, don't you think so? It seems to me he is at his best in that wonderful *adagio vivace* movement."

I must not forget to tell you that we have two new arrivals at the *pension*, namely, the Poet and his wife. I haven't the slightest idea what their name is except that it is very long and very unpronounceable. She is a dear little placid-faced woman of middle age, and he looks like one of Raphael's cherubs in twentieth century clothes. In spite of his infantile expression, however, I hear he has quite a reputation among men of letters.

A Fräulein Hartmann is expected to-morrow, and that will complete our household for the winter. She is the niece of Frau von Waldfel, who declares they greatly resemble each other. I can just imagine her: younger but with the same stout figure, rasping voice, and beady eyes! I do hope she won't be put next me at table.

To-day, while we were waiting in the salon for dinner to be announced, I chanced to play a few bars from a piece by MacDowell.

"Is that by your national composer, Sousa?" inquired Herr Doktor.

I hastily informed him that it was not.

"Why! I didn't know you had any other composers of importance," he remarked, with interest.

It is a sad but true fact that American music has, as yet, won no footing in Germany.

Wednesday.

This afternoon I had my first lesson with Thuille. I arrived just as the clock was striking two, and was shown at once into a large room, which in its furnishings and harmony of color betrays the artistic nature of its owner. An atmosphere of cigarette smoke hung about everything, and through the floating clouds by the windows I discerned Thuille just taking a final puff, tossing his cigarette away and coming to meet me with outstretched hand.

"*Ach! Guten Tag, Fräulein!*" he said, with a genial smile which put me instantly at my ease. Then he pulled forward a chair beside his own at the desk and bade me be seated. As I took my place a big white and brown hunting dog crawled out from the corner.

"This is my greatest pet," explained the professor, caressing the dog, who looked up with devoted eyes at his master's face. "I call him Tasso. Tasso, let me introduce you to a young American lady! Make a bow and then lie down."

Tasso obeyed in the cleverest fashion, Thuille watching him with pride. This introduction over, he turned to begin the lesson.

I had brought, as he requested, all the past work which I had with me, and he spent the entire hour in looking it over, asking questions and arranging a plan of study. I told him that I wanted that firm foundation which German thoroughness gives one, and he suggested that I begin by a review commencing with four-part choral writing, then simple counterpoint, and so on. This will form what I call the technical part of my study, and besides this I am to do a certain amount of free work and orchestration. Doesn't it sound interesting? I hurried home in a fever of impatience to begin the lesson he has given me for Saturday, only to find callers in the salon. They proved to be two New York girls, also music students. They are studying piano with Frau Langenhan-Hirzel, who is herself a pupil of Lescheticsky. Both are intensely enthusiastic over their work, and practise from five to six hours a day. After our coffee, Miss B—— offered to show me where her studio was, so, leaving her friend, who had a lesson, we walked down the Platz and up seven and ninety stairs to a tiny room under the eaves. It seems that Miss B—— is not allowed to practise in the *pension* where she lives, owing to the fact that three other students are singing, playing, or violin-scraping all day long, and the Frau landlady feared that another musician would banish utterly her supply of winter boarders. Hence Miss B—— was forced to seek a place to practise outside, and finally found a secluded room on the top floor of an old house at the very end of the Platz. In the subduing atmosphere of an undertaker's family she has made her musical home. The room is very small. One corner of the ceiling has caved in and threatens momentarily to fall. The only furniture is a cracked mirror, two rickety chairs, and a fine grand piano, which looks laughably out of place in these surroundings.

"There's only one thing that bothers me," she said, running over a bit of Chopin. "Just mark the effect of a *forte*." She played a crashing chord, and presto! the tiny, diamond panes of the windows rattled sharply in echo. Again a *sforzando* chord rang out, again came the jarring response.

"Isn't it awful?" she sighed. "My nerves are getting worn to shreds!"

Believe me, people at home don't know one half the trials of Munich music students.

October 20, 10.30 P. M.

To-night we made our first visit to the Hof-Theatre, which is the main opera house of the city, and heard Humperdinck's *Hänsel und Gretel*. I like the house immensely, its five balconies in white and gold are so impressive. The curtain is old rose in color, and on it the letter L is inscribed at intervals—for the unfortunate king, you know. What do you think I paid for my seat? Only fifty-five cents—and sat, too, in the orchestra. At the Conservatory last week I received an oblong bit of paper, a sort of certificate, which states that I am pursuing a course of musical study here. On presenting this at the box office I can get a seat in the rear of the parquet (which corresponds to our orchestra) for just half price. The seats do not extend under the balcony, so they are really very desirable. The extra five cents is for *Vorverkauft*, which means a fee for buying tickets in advance.

The opera itself is the most charming thing of its kind I have ever heard. The story is a fairy-tale concerning the delightful adventures of two children. Bosetti, a stout little German in spite of the Italian ring to her name, played Gretel and Fräulein Tordeck took the part of Hänsel. Both caught the spirit of the piece and sang and acted excellently. The music is fascinating in the extreme, and some of it—the prayer of the two mites in the wood, for example, which brought the tears to my eyes—very beautiful. There is no interruption. The music continues even during the pauses between the three so-called pictures of the opera. At the beginning of the second picture, which is laid in a wood, Gretel sings the loveliest solo, with the strings *pizzicato* and a flute obligato. Then there is a wonderful scene showing a flight of golden stairs thronged with white-robed angels who go up and down, while the children lie sleeping beneath a tree. If all the operas are produced as finely as this one I shall certainly think Germany the heaven of composers.

Yesterday Fräulein Hartmann, Frau von Waldfel's niece, arrived and proved a most agreeable surprise. Far from being what I had pictured, she is the prettiest creature imaginable, slight, with blue eyes, rosy cheeks, two fascinating dimples which come and go as she talks, and a bewildering profusion of light, fluffy hair which stubbornly refuses to remain in order, but curls about her head like a halo. Her aunt is immensely proud of her, although she treats her like a child. The chief cause of her pride seems to be that her niece is engaged—*verlobt*, as they say—to a German officer. You know it is considered *the* thing to marry into the army here, for it gives a woman at once the best social position, consequently all the young lieutenants are run after by diplomatic mammas and ambitious daughters, until I should think they would want to cry "Hold! Enough!" I believe the necessary dowry which the girl's parents pay over on the wedding day is twelve thousand marks, unless the bridegroom can show that he has that amount of money. It is, however, proverbial that the chief possession of a lieutenant are his unpaid bills, hence it seldom occurs that he himself can afford to marry at his own free will.

Fräulein Hartmann, while essentially German in type, has an unusually sweet expression characterized by a curious little droop at the corners of her mouth which puzzles me a bit. I am sure it is not the result of a spoiled nature, for her patience with her aunt's querulousness belies that, but it seems rather the expression which we associate with unhappiness or pain. At any rate she is decidedly the most interesting person in the *pension*, and I hope to know her better.

Six o'clock.

The day is dying royally, and as I look out across the now brown and barren tree-tops of the Platz, I see a sky which is one blaze of glory. There is always music in the clouds. Have you never heard the tender, inspiring melody in soft, fleecy puffs as they float in a sea of azure—or caught the melancholy strains of 'cello and oboe in lowering gray masses against a background darker still? On an afternoon like this, surely you have thrilled in response to the piercing cry of trumpets, horns, and trombones, in the riotous masses of scarlet, violet, and gold which flood the heaven? It does not last long, this intoxicating draught of color and melody, for, as I watch, the clouds dissolve with the resolution of a chord. I can hear the *diminuendo rallentando* of the orchestra as the gold dulls, the scarlet fades to rose, the rose to pink. It hovers—this last, long streak—in one delicate flush against the violet sky, while the strings sustain *pianissimo* the tonic harmony. Then it suddenly dies, and the music with it. The day is done.

III

MUNICH, *November 8.*

Behold me recovering this morning from the effects of my first participation in German frivolity. The occasion was the *Namens-Tag* (name day) of the Baroness.

"You see to-day is mother's saint's day, the one for whom she was named," explained Karl, not very clearly, at dinner.

"Is it the custom to celebrate this instead of the birthday?" I inquired.

Karl looked at me with an expression of pity at my ignorance.

"We always have a fête on *both* days," he said, "with extra wine and a lot of grand things to eat."

"Yes, indeed," said the Baroness, beaming from her end of the table.

"Yes, indeed," echoed the Baron, beaming back on her and radiating his delight along the line of *pensionnaires* each side. The eyes of Herr Doktor twinkled as he looked across at me. I met his glance with a half smile. Neither of us meant to be unkind. France and America were merely united in their appreciation of the humorous. Frau von Waldfel raised her eyebrows disagreeably, and looked as though about to start a discussion. To mention food in the presence of that woman is like brandishing a red flag before a bull. Luckily Herr Doktor saw the signs of approaching storm, and with his usual diplomacy turned the trend of conversation, so that an argument was averted for this meal at least.

Is there anything more pitiable than a number of guests, hitherto unknown to one another, endeavoring to appear at ease as they wait the summons to dinner? We had thought to avoid this situation by not appearing till half after seven that evening, the hour set for the supper party. Imagine, then, our feelings, when fifteen minutes, a half hour, three quarters dragged by, and no vestige of life from the dining-room! Everything moves slowly in Germany, and the culinary department is no exception. The Baroness never seemed so much like a beneficent angel as when she opened the dining-room door and invited us to the table. And now a light shone through the clouds, for the stupid Count with whom I had been struggling to converse was whisked away to the other end of the table, and Lieutenant Linder, a young man of about seven and twenty, in the dark blue and scarlet uniform of Bavaria, took the place on my left.

Oh, these officers! They simply own Munich. When they stride along the street, the entire sidewalk is their undisputed possession. How their swords clank, how faultlessly their jackets fit, how their heavenward-pointing mustaches curl! A few of them are really handsome, but if not, it doesn't matter in the slightest. The resplendency of their uniforms would make one forgive almost anything. When I became accustomed to the atmosphere of conceit in which Lieutenant Linder was enveloped, I found him distinctly entertaining, and, better yet, he had a sense of humor. What with his helping me with my German, and my giving him a lesson in English, we managed to get on famously.

The table was profusely decorated with flowers, and there was a great deal to eat and more to drink. The idea in cooking seems to be to produce a color effect. For example, we had as one course well-browned sausage surrounded by a mass of bright red carrots. Next came the eternal veal, reposing in a vivid green sea of spinach. Do your æsthetic sensibilities shrink at these materialistic descriptions? Remember I am in a materialistic land, amid a materialistic people. Truly the problem which continually confronts me is: how can a people who seem so lethargic, and who make no disguise of their love for the product of the soil and the grape, produce such marvellous, almost superhuman results in the fields of music and philosophy?

I might have meditated at some length on this question during the *Namens-Tag* supper, had not the Lieutenant kept up a rapid conversation, for we were at the table until half-past eleven. Not that we were eating all the time, but the waits between the courses were very long, and in the middle of the dinner we had a pause of twenty minutes—like an intermission at an assembly—when the Poet, with marked nervousness, read some original verses "To the Baroness on her Name-Day." The poor woman was even more embarrassed than he, and so moved, when at the close we all rose to drink her health, that two large tears ran down her fat cheeks.

"*Hoch soll sie leben!*" cried Herr Doktor, clinking his glass to mine. Every one had to touch his glass to every one else's or it was "no fair," and of course we all walked up to the Baroness and touched hers.

When the coffee had at last been served, we went into the salon carrying away with us a glass of *Bowle*, or punch, which is much milder than anything called by that name in America. In came a round little man who took his place at the piano, and dancing began.

Lieutenant Linder, with an extremely low bow, begged *gnädiges Fräulein* to give him the honor of the first waltz. *Gnädiges Fräulein* consented, and off we started. The floor was excellent,—you know one finds hardwood floors everywhere here instead of carpets,—but oh, how fast these Germans dance! The Lieutenant swung me round and round in a small circle, *prestissimo*, until I begged him to stop, whereupon he looked very much surprised and asked me if I had heart trouble. I assured him that such was not the case, but that we were not accustomed in America to whirl about like tops.

Waltzes and old-fashioned polkas followed in rapid succession. I can't imagine how *Herr Leutnant* ever managed to do that one-two-three-hop, one-two-three-hop, without falling over his sword. At midnight everybody, including Frau von Waldfel, danced the *Française*, which is much like our Virginia Reel. You should have seen how the Baron and Baroness enjoyed it, and how astonishingly light they were on their feet! They fairly glowed with pleasure, and reminded me of Mr. and Mrs. Fessiwig at the Christmas party.

I had looked forward to this affair with considerable curiosity, not only because it was to be my first glimpse of German social life, but also because the Baroness had invited Lieutenant Blum, the *fiancé* of Fräulein Hartmann. I must confess, however, that I was much disappointed in him. He is short and dark, with a heavy, black mustache which he constantly caresses with his fat little hands. Although I did not exchange a word with him the whole evening, except the formalities of an introduction, I could not shake off the impression that he was of much coarser fibre than his betrothed. However, he paid her the most devoted attention the entire evening, and is, apparently, very much in love.

At one o'clock *Mütterchen* and I exchanged glances. I had a lesson at the Conservatory the next morning at nine. But at the first hint of our leaving, the Baroness looked so distressed and surprised that we were afraid we had been very rude and determined to do the proper thing. The proper thing in this instance meant staying up to dance till half-past four in the morning. Oh! how sleepy I was as I crept into bed and thanked my stars that the *Namens-Tag fête* was over.

Evening.

By this time I am beginning to feel quite like a native. My surroundings no longer seem strange. I am growing accustomed to five meals a day and the language sounds fairly rational. My work has settled into a regular routine. The entire mornings are devoted to study. In the afternoons come lessons. Twice a week I have a private lesson with Thuille. At the Conservatory I am studying singing with Frau Bianci and piano with Fräulein Fischer, which makes four lessons more. The piano lessons are in a class with two other girls, and not as formidable as you might suppose, for I have explained to Fräulein Fischer that I am only including piano to keep from forgetting what I already know, and that I need most of my time on my composition lessons with Thuille. She is very kind, and every two weeks we are to read duets together. This makes six lessons a week, and what with the score-reading class and the chorus, I see a busy winter before me. The singing and piano lessons are given in a large, imposing room. It contains two grand pianos and is furnished in red velvet. I could hardly reconcile this with my ideas of a Conservatory, but Frau Bianci explained that the building was originally used for something quite different. Just fancy—we address all the teachers by titles! "Herr Professor" falls now quite trippingly from my tongue, and even "Frau Professor," but "Fräulein Professor" is a little too much for me as yet!

I will acknowledge that I felt rather strange at the first meeting of the score-reading class, when, on entering the room with the score of Haydn's symphonies under my arm, I encountered the astonished gaze of thirty pairs of masculine eyes. You could have heard a pin drop, the place was so still, as I walked by the different groups and took a seat near the window. Then a low whispering started among the students. Evidently I had created a sensation. A moment later the big door opened and Stavenhagen came in. Every one rose, or straightened himself up at once. With a nod which seemed to include us all, the director took his seat by the piano and the lesson began. Each one was called on to play a number of bars written in four different clefs, the old soprano, the tenor, the alto, and the bass—Stavenhagen selecting a new choral every time. It was not till near the end of the hour that he called my name. Just as I took my seat before the keyboard, feeling intensely nervous and fearing lest my fingers tremble visibly, I heard one of the men smother a laugh. That settled it! I was bound to do or die, and with a calmness quite unnatural I played the bars set before me without a mistake. Nobody laughed when I had finished, and now that the first shock is over, the students treat me with the utmost courtesy. Indeed, they seem to have accepted me as inevitable, although occasionally I catch one of them staring at me with an expression which says as plainly as words, "What on earth does a woman want of score reading?"

The chorus is well under way. To-day is Thursday, and while you have been singing with the faithful in the Cecilia Society I, too, have been at a rehearsal, only we call it a *Probe* here, and the atmosphere is somewhat different from that of Pilgrim Hall. The *Oberster Chor* (which means the upper chorus) met at five o'clock to-day. The room where we sit is on the top floor and at the end is an organ. I think the orchestra class generally practises here. The air is always frightfully close and hot, for there are about two hundred of us and never a window open. That is the German idea. What a splendid thing a Fresh Air Fund would be over here!

The piano against the wall is on a raised platform about which the chorus forms a half circle. Professor Becht, one of the organ teachers, presides. Such a time as he does have endeavoring to maintain order! But the moment we begin to sing—ah! that is a different matter. Each pupil becomes utterly absorbed in the notes before him, from the first measure to the last. Each sings as though he loves to sing; yes, better than that, as though he actually feels what he sings, which is more than can be said of many vocalists who have won both fame and fortune. There, you see, is another side of these complex Germans. The love of music is their birthright, the appreciation of it intuitive.

How I wish you might see some of this queer congregation! The masculine element ranges from small boys to bearded men. The girls and men are kept strictly separate, like the sheep and the goats. They enter and go out by different doors, for the building is divided in two distinct sections. The sanctity of each section is kept as inviolate as a Shaker settlement.

The front row of tenors in the chorus amuses me exceedingly. It consists of boys who wear their hair pompadour and yell outrageously. Did you ever notice the effect of a boy with pompadour hair opening his mouth very wide? It is truly startling. The basses form a curious *vis-à-vis* for these youthful aspirants. Their age is in the neighborhood of thirty. Obviously to be a bass singer requires both dignity and experience. Most of them think it also requires a full beard. Several of the pupils affect the artistic, or are dressed after the old masters, with long hair, brown corduroy velvet jackets, and flowing neckties. There is one I have named Rubenstein, he looks so much like the pictures of the great pianist. And the most interesting tenor-boy I call Beethoven. He wears a big white collar into which he sinks his chin, and with deep, earnest eyes under closely knit brows gazes gravely out on a frivolous world.

I felt very much like the proverbial stray cat as I entered the room at the first rehearsal, alone and silent in all that crowd of chattering German girls. Not knowing where to sit, I cast an anxious look around and caught the friendly glance of a girl in the second row. She beckoned to me somewhat shyly.

"There is a place here, if you care for it," she said.

Overjoyed to hear my mother tongue, I gladly took the seat beside her, and we were soon chatting in the unconventional way known to strangers who meet on strange soil. I could not but notice with what a high-bred manner my new friend carried her head. Her hair, black and curling, is coiled in a low knot at the back of the whitest of necks, for she wears her blouses cut out a little without a collar, as is the strange and rather chilling fashion here. I was struck, too, by her jacket of black velvet, an odd school dress, but one which seems to suit her perfectly.

"You are English, are you not?" I questioned.

"Not at all," said she, her blue eyes snapping as much as blue eyes ever can snap. "I'm Irish. I come from County Cork."

"Oh!" I said, drawing a long breath, as visions of the representatives County Cork generally sends to America flashed through my mind.

"I'm taking piano as my *Hauptsache* with Krause," she went on. "You know Stavenhagen and Krause have a great many foreign pupils. By the bye," she continued, "I have a friend myself in the United States. I wonder if you know her—a Miss Curtis."

"Couldn't you tell me what city she lives in?" I suggested. "I know several people of that name."

"Then I'm sure you know her. How delightful!" she replied, radiant. (I made a mental note of the fact that jumping at conclusions is a trait not confined exclusively to American women.) "She comes from Los Angeles."

For the twentieth time since my arrival in Munich I explained the relative situation of Boston and San Francisco, and politely regretted that I could not know all the music students as far as the Pacific coast.

I was surprised at first to see how much deference is paid the professors here. Whenever one enters the room we all immediately rise and do not sit until he either goes out or, by a gracious wave of the hand, accords us permission to resume our places. In spite of my democratic birth, these marks of respect impressed me as extremely fitting. About every two weeks comes a "*Vortragsabend*," an evening devoted to a concert by the pupils. Stavenhagen has a large orchestra composed of the students, which he conducts himself. We are marked, too, by some occult system whereby our standing is never known unless we "flunk."

Last week I had a very pleasant chat with Professor Gluth. He is a well-known composer here, has written several operas, and teaches at the school. Margaret Ruthven Lang had been kind enough to give me a letter of introduction to him. He was her teacher when she was in Munich. I have been trying to see him for some time, but have always missed him. He is a splendid-looking man, very large, with white hair, and his manner is most cordial. He was delighted to hear of Miss Lang, and I was proud to tell him of her success in the musical world.

We have been to the opera twice since I wrote, once to hear *Die Weisse Dame* and the second to hear "Fidelio." I am afraid the report that the Prince Regent was to be there had more to do with our going than the desire to hear *Die Weisse Dame* itself, although it is a pretty opera in its way. The audience was very splendid and the royal box brilliantly lighted. The most expensive places are in the first balcony, and here we saw very fine costumes and jewels. At ten minutes past seven—the opera as a rule begins at seven—the orchestra struck up "God save the King," and the people rose *en masse* as the Prince, accompanied by the Crown Princess and several members of the royal family, entered the box. The Regent at once came to the front, and with one hand resting on the red velvet railing, bowed repeatedly to right and left.

He is of medium height, with white hair and flowing white beard. His eyes are bright and kindly, and his bearing, while most dignified, is utterly without ostentation. It was an inspiring sight,—the five balconies, the floor, and the boxes all alive with a crowd of enthusiastic people, who, standing, faced this man who served them as king, and applauded till the house echoed with their cries of "*Hoch! Hoch!*"

Although "Fidelio," which we heard on Wednesday, presented no such gorgeous spectacle, how much more we enjoyed that evening! Morena sang the title rôle, and I feel as though I never want to see any one else in the part. She is a tall, commanding woman of great beauty, and the masculine dress of Leonora suits her marvellously. Her voice is exquisite, fresh, and true, and her acting shows great intensity of power and feeling. Bosetti, who, you remember, sang so delightfully in *Hänsel und Gretel* made a charming Marzelline. When the opera was over *Mütterchen* and I rose to go, but to our surprise saw that the audience remained seated. As we took our places again, Zumpe raised his baton and the first measures of that divine Leonore overture number three rang out. I have never heard anything more impressive, coming as it did to form a finale to the opera itself. It seemed as though the people held their breath during the performance; not a rustle, not a movement distracted one from the glorious music of the orchestra. At the close the whole house broke into wild applause and cries for "Zumpe! Zumpe!"

I do think this German enthusiasm splendid. We talk about the stolidity of the Teutonic race, but I have never yet seen here an unresponsive audience. If they do not like a thing they remain silent. It is the exception to hear any hissing, although it now and then occurs. If they do like a thing they applaud, and applaud lustily. They resemble big, impulsive children, and the man who said "There is nothing for preserving the body like having no heart" would find no place among them. That cherished enormity known as Modern Indifference, by so many of us regarded as the outward sign of culture, is, in Germany, thank Heaven, conspicuous by its absence.

November 28.

Yesterday was Thanksgiving Day. I could hardly realize that you were feasting at home on turkey and cranberry sauce amid all the festivities of the season. The day here passed as usual with my morning of study and a lesson with Thuille in the afternoon. In the evening, that we might not forget what day it was, the American colony had a dinner and dance at one of the large hotels. I had no idea before that there were so many Americans in Munich. Colonel W—— said there must be about four hundred in all, and fully two hundred and fifty came to the dinner. The rooms were lavishly decorated with American flags and flowers, as were also the tables. And oh! how pleasant was the sound of English on every side. The consul's wife and the rector's wife received the guests under a red, white, and blue bower, and at seven o'clock we all went into the dining-room to the strains of the "Star Spangled Banner." The rector asked grace and then came the dinner. That, dear Cecy, I must confess, was but a farce when compared to the genuine creation, in spite of the American flag on the menu and the assurance that these were American turkeys especially imported for the occasion. The cranberry sauce, too, would, I believe, have been passed by unrecognized on the other side, but anything was preferable to dining on veal and beer on Thanksgiving Day. After the dinner came dancing—it had been thought best to have no speeches—and it did seem delightful to trip it in a sane way once more. The whole affair was decidedly successful, and made us realize that Thanksgiving was a real institution even if we were on German soil.

I must tell you how charming all the people here made my birthday, which came this week. In the morning *Mütterchen* presented me with some lovely gifts tied with a red, white, and blue ribbon. To our surprise, about ten o'clock came a knock on my door, and in walked Karl bearing a huge cake on a tray, the Baron and Baroness following. They were all three beaming with delight, and each shook my hand a dozen times in their cordial way, wishing me all sorts of good things. The cake had been ordered and made at the pastry cook's especially for me. It was round and bore across the top, in letters of marvellous white frosting script, "*Herzlichen Gruss*" (Hearty Greeting).

"That must have the place of honor," I cried, much moved by their friendliness, as I swept the books off the table. "It is truly a wonderful cake."

Hardly had they gone when a second knock sounded, and in response to my "*Herein!*" in came the servants in a row, headed by Georg, the butler. Twisting the buttons of his livery, he made a little speech very fast, all of which I could not understand, but the burden of it was a wish that the *lieber Gott* would keep *gnädiges Fräulein* in health and happiness all her days. Then he shook me warmly by the hand. The maids followed, each wishing me good fortune in some pretty couplet, and with a quaint little courtesy also shaking my hand. It was all done with such delightful simplicity that I can never forget it.

But this was not all the kindness I received, for when we went out to dinner, there on my plate was a beautiful basket of white roses from my "friends in the *pension*." I did not know what to say in my surprise, so I only exclaimed *Danke Tausendmal* (a thousand thanks), and sat down quickly, lest I should cry or do some equally foolish thing.

Just as we were leaving the room after dinner Frau von Waldfel came up to me, her niece by her side.

"I want to tell you, my dear, that I sent to Nuremberg for some *Lebkuchen* in honor of your birthday," she said. "You will find the package in your room. They tried to persuade me in the shops," she added, lowering her voice to a whisper, "that the *Lebkuchen* they sell here are as good as the genuine article, but I know better, and these are the real Nuremberg ones, famous the world over."

I thanked her heartily for her thoughtfulness, assuring her that I had often read of them in my fairy-tale books. Then they both shook hands and Fräulein Hartmann, blushing slightly, leaned over and kissed me.

"It is the custom," she said shyly, "and perhaps you will miss your American friends less on this day if you realize you have made new ones here." Wasn't it sweet of her?

In the evening we celebrated by going to the *Populäres Konzert*—the Baron and Baroness, Herr Doktor, Lieutenant Linder, *Mütterchen*, and myself. It was held in the Kaim Saal, where the Weingartner concerts are given, and rendered by the same orchestra under the leadership of Scharrer. In place of the rows of seats were substituted tables as at our "Pops" at home. The hall was extremely crowded when we entered and we did not at first obtain a table where we could sit together. *Mütterchen* and I took places at one in the rear, and I noticed after we had been seated a few moments the disagreeable expression on the faces of the strangers at the table. In fact, two of them looked seriously offended and made some remark to each other, *sotto voce*, with a glance towards us. In bewilderment I wondered what could have destroyed their equanimity, for they seemed placid enough when we first came in. Suddenly it flashed across me.

"Don't you remember," I whispered to *Mütterchen*, "Edith told us the other day it was the custom to bow to those sitting at table whenever we took a seat with them? We didn't do it, hence this atmosphere of ungracious toleration."

Mütterchen looked alarmed, but just then the lieutenant came up to take us to a table large enough for our whole party, and we soothed the wounded feelings of those we had so unconsciously offended by bestowing the most cordial of bows as we went away.

This was not, however, our only unhappy experience, born of ignorance and American training, on that evening. It chanced, when we reached home after the concert, that the lieutenant turned to *Mütterchen* first to say good night.

"A most enjoyable evening, *gnädige Frau*," he said, bending low over her hand. That he was to kiss it she had not the slightest premonition. In point of fact he didn't, but he tried to, while *Mütterchen* innocently raised her hand at the critical moment and gave him a fearful rap under the nose. His glasses flew off with a crash, and he flushed very red, more from the blow than embarrassment. It takes a great deal to embarrass a German officer. While he groped about on the floor in search of his glasses, *Mütterchen* stammered forth a flood of apologies in the best German the Berlitz School affords. We were indeed relieved when he recovered the glasses intact, and a hearty laugh banished our distress, for the Germans like a joke—provided it is not too subtle—as well as the rest of us.

Wagner's Ring of the Nibelungen is to be given in two weeks, and we purchased our seats to-day. I am all enthusiasm to hear it and am reading the poems. I have a splendid little book which has the leading motifs written out at the back and in the margins of the pages a statement of just what motif occurs at certain lines. It sounds complex,—doesn't it?—but is most interesting. Wish me joy, and in the meantime believe me, as always,

M.

P. S. Fräulein Hartmann is not happy. I am convinced of it. To be sure, I never see her except at table, for her aunt keeps her always closely by her side. But to-day I passed the girl in the hall, and her eyes were swollen from crying. She looked so sad that I stopped and asked her if I could not do something for her. For a moment she looked at me hesitatingly and seemed about to speak, when in walked her unbearable aunt.

"My niece has a frightful headache," she exclaimed, "and bed is the best place for her."

I feel sure that odious lieutenant has been doing or not doing something that disturbs her. I am constantly meeting him on the stairs. He comes in every day to drink afternoon coffee and is usually sauntering down just as I come in from the chorus hour at the Conservatory. When he sees me he bows very low, and, with a twist of his tiresome mustache and a glance which he imagines is impressive, hopes "*sehr geehrtes Fräulein* is in good health."

If it weren't for his stunning uniform I don't believe the pretty Fräulein would look at him twice!

IV

MUNICH, *December 8.*

Dear Cecilia:—

The wind is shrieking in great gusts, which begin *piano, crescendo* to *fortissimo,* and then die away in weird, unearthly echoes, while the rain keeps up a continuous counterpoint to this minor music in sharp *staccato* against the window panes. The mist is so thick that the obelisk at the end of Max-Josephstrasse looks like a mere shadow. It is now five o'clock and I have "shut up shop," as it were, to talk with you, for my lesson for to-morrow, a fugue in C minor, is finished. It occurred to me, as I was writing it, how curiously a fugue subject resembles certain clever and unscrupulous people. Both are thoroughly adaptable, both are capable of saying the direct opposite of what they have previously boldly stated, both are difficult to deal with and can only be managed successfully by employing the greatest finesse.

Tuesday.

I was interrupted in my letter of yesterday by Frau von Waldfel and her niece, who came to call. Of course that meant a cup of coffee. When they left I had to hurry down to the school for a lesson, so writing was out of the question. By the bye, I am afraid I may have excited your sympathies unduly in favor of Fräulein Hartmann, for ever since that day I wrote you, when I met her crying in the hall, she has appeared most cheerful. Yesterday she was in unusual spirits, although to tell the truth her gayety struck me as somewhat forced. It was as if she were endeavoring to overcome the impression which her tears must have given me.

After my lesson with Thuille yesterday I stopped in at Miss Pollard's. She is a piano student with whom I have become acquainted, and goes by the nickname of Polly. I found her sitting on a very low stool before the piano and resting her fingers on the keys, for all the world like a child too little to reach up to play.

"What *are* you doing?" I said.

"I'm practising," she said, with crushing dignity. Then, throwing me a supercilious glance, "This is an exercise especially recommended by Lescheticsky."

"Oh!" said I meekly, inwardly wondering if there are any more sensitive creatures on earth than we music students. How enthusiastically we rave over our "method"! How more than ready we are to challenge man, woman, or child who breathes a doubt of its infallibility! And oh! with what majestic disdain we utterly ignore the very existence of any other! Realizing all this, I judged it wiser to change the subject by asking quickly,—

"Are the girls coming to-day?"

No sooner had I spoken than in came the two New York girls of whom I wrote as calling on me when I first arrived. We have become firm friends by this time. Over a cup of tea we four discussed the last Weingartner concert, and more especially Alexander Petschnikof. (I can never pronounce his name without wanting to sneeze.) He had played the Mozart Concerto and Bach's Chiaconna most acceptably, to judge from his reception. Since none of us were violinists we felt free to discuss his style and phrasing with all that intolerance which people are wont to employ when criticising things of which they themselves are ignorant.

Just as we were putting on our wraps Polly made a confession.

"Well, girls, I'll have to tell you the truth," she said. "I've been complained of to the police."

"Again?" said Louise, in a startled whisper.

"Again?" Edith and I echoed, aghast.

"And who is it this time?" demanded Edith. She has a way of recovering and getting at the root of things before any one else. She did not ask why. We all knew that there could be but one reason. Polly, usually the essence of demureness, turned and looked at us with hard, angry eyes.

"It's the Poet downstairs," she explained. "He says I'm ruining his inspirations by my barbaric pounding. Fancy that reaching Lescheticsky's ears! He says I'm 'at it' all day!"

"Outrageous!" cried Louise.

"Preposterous!" avowed Edith.

They were both following the laws of Lescheticsky.

"I'm so sorry," said I more mildly, for somehow I could not help but see a picture of the distressed poet, pacing the floor, and beating his brow as he vainly sought for a brilliant thought, while from above came the unceasing, monotonous, nerve-destroying sound of a Czerny exercise repeated over and over.

"It's not the moving I mind," continued Polly, "I'm quite an adept at that, having lived in three *pensions* since my arrival last August." Here she smiled bitterly. "But at one thing I do rebel, and that is at having to pay thirty marks for a damper for my piano, which I ordered from Berlin in the hope of appeasing him when he complained a week ago!"

It was, indeed, an unhappy situation. We all knew, too, that those thirty marks meant a good deal to Polly.

"Perhaps, after all, it will come out all right," said Louise consolingly.

"I consider it an absolutely absurd proceeding!" said Edith emphatically, as she stamped out into the hall.

"You might come down and talk with the Poet's Wife at our *pension*," I suggested. We always said "the Poet's Wife," since we had long ago given up her five-syllable name as hopeless. "I'm sure she would be able to help you."

You see Polly lives alone. We three discussed the matter as we walked down the Ludwig-strasse, the girls leaving me at the Conservatory, where I had a piano lesson at five.

And now I must stop, for it is time to dress for the opera. To think of hearing the "Rheingold" at last!

Saturday.

I have heard the "Rheingold" and "The Valkyrie," and can hardly wait for "Siegfried" to-morrow night. Every seat in the Hof-Theatre was occupied, and an immense crowd stood downstairs. The price of seats, increased three marks, seemed to make no difference in the attendance. Polly and two of her friends were too late to obtain any desirable places, so they clubbed together and engaged a *Dienstmann* to get their seats for them. One finds a *Dienstmann* at every turning here. They are forlorn, sad-eyed creatures, in short, frayed jackets and red caps, who linger on street corners gazing abstractedly into space with their hands in their pockets. For a small sum they will run from one end of Munich to the other, or, if need be, will stand in line for tickets from four in the morning on. Polly has a favorite old *Dienstmann* called Friedrich. Accordingly, Friedrich was summoned to the rescue and stood the entire night with hundreds of others on the chilly stones of Max-Joseph-Platz in order to get seats. There is a rule that not more than three tickets can be sold to one of these men. The places in the gallery cost two marks (fifty cents) and the *Dienstmann* demands, for standing all night, generally four marks. It is divided among the trio, so they get their places for about eighty cents. This price is the exception, however; ordinarily one pays but thirty-five cents for a seat at this altitude.

When it comes to sitting in the balcony or orchestra one finds that the fabulous stories which one hears in America about the cheapness of opera are grossly exaggerated.

"Why, opera costs nothing over there!" you hear. "One can go for a song!"

As a matter of fact, the seats in the first balcony generally cost two dollars, an orchestra seat a dollar and a half, and very often these prices are considerably increased.

Is there anything more exquisite than the first act of the "Rheingold," more bewitching than those elusive daughters of the Rhine, more perfect than the enchantment of those rippling chords? The whole scene is a flawless poem. When it came to the second act, however, my indomitable sense of humor rose to the surface. You have heard that old adage, haven't you, "Laugh and the world laughs with you, weep and you weep alone"? I have proven satisfactorily that the first part is a fallacy pure and simple—at least in Germany. Was I at fault because when I first heard the giant motif I smiled? Am I to be condemned because I had to smother a laugh when Mimi rolled over and over on the stage, and shrieked forth a ridiculous "Augh!" as in a fit of indigestion? And the giants were such wild-looking creatures with grotesque tufts of hair on the crown of their heads—should I have taken them more seriously? Apparently, if I am to judge from the demeanor of the audience, who never changed their expression during the entire opera. And, after all, there are a good many people at home who think to regard one bar of Wagner without reverential seriousness is sacrilege. Yet "to thine own self be true," Cecilia, and so I make no defence. What need when I am writing to one who Understands?

The spring motif of "The Valkyrie" is the incarnation of tenderness and eternal freshness, and the climax of the whole opera seems to me simply colossal. Brünnhilde, sung by Senger-Bettaque, was convincing and forceful. Her supposedly fiery steed, a raw-boned black creature who looked sufficiently mild for children to drive, was reluctantly dragged in, licking sugar in a most obvious fashion from the corners of his mouth. Even a sturdy and belligerent Brünnhilde, it seems, must at times yield to puerile means in order to gain her point. Later the war-maiden was seen scudding through the sky on a snow-white charger, so I judged she must have been fortunate enough to exchange her apathetic beast during the course of the opera. Fricka was sung by Fräulein Fremstad, whose Carmen, I hear, has made quite a furore. The whole thing was splendidly given, and in the last act I gleaned considerable knowledge about the bass tuba which comes in here so often, just as in the "Rheingold" I marked the growling themes for 'cello and double basses.

Monday.

Well, it's all over, that wonderful Ring! "Siegfried" came on Thursday, and Knote, whom I had previously heard as Tristan, sang the title rôle. At the end of the first act the audience fairly went wild with enthusiasm. Oh, that wonderful bit of orchestration where Mimi speaks of fear! And that perfect effect of the bird-voice in the *Waldweben*, singing in the clarinet above the strings, while the horn note, *pianissimo*, gives that poignant touch of color which only the brain of a master could conceive.

The dragon, which Herr Martens tells me is generally a small affair, was horrible and immense enough for any one. I positively trembled when he poured forth clouds of steam from his gaping jaws, and disclosed a throat of red fire. The bass tuba makes a grand worm. I never realized what it was to hear a worm crawl before. But in spite of the wonders of the work, I wish it were shorter. My head was frightfully tired endeavoring to follow the countless interwoven themes. But then, this is my first hearing of it all, and perhaps another time I might change my opinion.

What a stupendous climax *Gotterdammerung* is to the whole Ring! The prelude is perfect, and I can imagine no more dramatic moment than that when Siegfried drinks to Brünnhilde in the fatal draught. Never shall I forget the grandeur of the music at the breaking of day, before the entrance of the hero, and the stirring sound of those eight horns; nor will that last grand picture of Valhalla fade from my mind for many moons.

It seemed as though half the American colony had turned out for the Ring, for we continually met people we knew at the intermissions. There is always a pause of twenty minutes at some time between the acts. Why, you inquire? My dear Cecilia, a German would never think of existing two hours without refreshment, much less four; consequently there isn't a theatre or opera house in all Germany which does not contain a restaurant. To be sure, it is rather a come-down to discover Professor B——, whom you saw a moment ago enthralled by the strains of the *Waldweben*, now prosaically munching a ham-sandwich and drinking beer in a corner of the café, as though his soul had never been stirred beyond the excitement of choosing what he should order for dinner. But that is the German temperament, and one soon gets used to it.

There is the "Siegfried" bird-call running through my head again! Is it that which the fountain—my fountain, as I claim it now—sang to me as I passed to-day? Or did I myself unconsciously hum the melody and hear in the ripple of the falling water the soft rhythm of accompanying 'cellos and violins?

December 15.

Christmas is in the air, and every street-corner has bloomed into a miniature forest of trees. These are fastened in squares of wood, and stand up straight and proud. As a rule some strange, bent old woman presides over them, and out of curiosity to-day I stopped in Odeons-Platz and inquired the price of a particularly plump little tree.

"One mark fifty" (thirty-seven and a half cents), quavered the dame, "but they run up as high as fifteen marks."

The poor soul looked so disappointed as I, after thanking her, turned away, that I simply could not resist going back—least of all at Christmas time. There was nothing to buy but trees, so I picked out the plump little one which had first attracted my attention. She was delighted and beamed at me as I started off with it dragging behind me from under my arm, for my hands were full of music books. I had not the slightest idea what to do with my new possession. I had just made up my mind to leave it at some one's door, when who should come trudging along through the snow but the Hausmeister's little boy. He was on his way home from school, with his books strapped to his back in one of these curious black knapsacks which all the school children carry. I thrust the tree into his arms, with the assurance that it was for him, and left him, wholly bewildered, hugging it tightly to his breast.

When I reached the corner I turned to see him still standing there and gazing after me from between the branches with an expression of astonishment and delight. I waved my hand, and at last he moved and gave a sign with his red mitten. Then he turned and ran towards home as fast as his fat legs could carry him.

The shops, with one exception, are not nearly as finely decorated as ours at home. This exception is the sausage-store, which is a thing of beauty and a joy forever. To be frank, a sausage had never impressed me as a particularly artistic creation, nor had I been wont to regard it as a species of decoration until Germany unfolded to me its many possibilities. Could you but see one of these windows, hung with long ropes, the links of which are large Frankfurters joined together by a band of green, you would not fail, I am sure, to admire the intricacy of the designs and the striking originality with which the small sausages are interspersed with the larger ones so as to produce the most surprising effects! Who ever associated sausages with anything so idyllic as a waterfall? Yet here you have a wooden mill, high up on an improvised hill, and over the wheel flow down streamers of sausages to mass in a lake below. Who ever thought of connecting them with the legends of the Middle Ages? Yet Herr Schmidt, at the corner, has constructed the most marvellous tower out of sausages laid crisscross, with openings for little windows, with a turret on the very top, with a flag waving proudly on the highest peak, and most wonderful of all, with a drawbridge securely fastened over a moat of parsley.

Everybody gives every one else some little remembrance for Christmas, and we are racking our brains to think of things appropriate for those at the *pension*. The clerks in the shops help one out all they can. You have no idea how courteous they are. Always on entering they say "Good day" and the proprietor comes up with "How can I serve you, *gnädiges Fräulein?*" Then they will pull down all the goods in the store, bring out hidden boxes from under the counters, and even send outside for something they have not got, remaining perfectly satisfied if you only purchase something. If you buy nothing, however politely you may regret that the silk does not match, or the lace bear the required pattern, they plainly show their displeasure in their faces.

We are always politely escorted to the door by a clerk, who bids us good by. Often in the smaller stores it is amusing to hear the chorus of farewells which follow us. Last week Polly and I had coffee at one of these fascinating *Conditorei*, or little bake-shops which one finds here everywhere. For an absurdly small sum we had a table to ourselves, coffee enough for a dozen, and the most delicious cakes you ever ate! When we had finished, I started to leave some *Trinkgeld* for the waitress, who had served everything in the daintiest fashion.

"Fifty pfennigs!" said Polly, looking at the coin that I had laid on the table.

"I felt I ought to give more, but they told me——" I began.

"More!" exclaimed Polly. "I never heard of such a thing! Don't you know that ten pfennigs (two cents and a half) for each person is considered quite sufficient?"

Polly has lived here longer than I, and has absorbed the idea that a pfennig—a fifth of a cent—is a pfennig, and not to be lightly treated. Accordingly I laid the sum on the table. The waitress swept the money into the black leather bag which she wore about her waist just as Kathie does in *Alt-Heidelberg*, and expressed her thanks repeatedly as she opened the door for us to pass out.

"*Bitte, verehren uns wieder!*" (Please honor us again) said the proprietor from her desk.

"*Adieu, meine Damen,*" cried the waitress at the table in the corner, while our little maid poured forth a continual sing song of "*Danke sehr, meine Damen. Besten Dank! Habe die Ehre!*" (I have the honor) until we were out on the street.

Polly and I looked at each other and laughed.

"Don't fancy it was the effect of the tip," said she. "They go through the same program for half the money. I always give ten pfennigs and have never missed a word."

She laughed again gaily, for she is once more quite happy inasmuch as the "poet on the floor below" has been suddenly called to Stuttgart. A drama of his has been accepted there, and he was so overcome with joy that he withdrew his complaint and told Polly she might "bang away" till he returned.

"And now come down to the Schlüssel Bazar with me," she said, tucking my hand coaxingly under her arm. "I want you to help me select a gift."

There is no more fascinating place for a Christmas shopper than the Bazar, but I glanced at the clock on the Theatiner church.

"I really can't, Polly," I said; "there is a chorus rehearsal at five, the last before the concert, and I must hurry along this minute or I shall be late."

So we parted, and I wended my way quickly through the fast-gathering dusk, past the Feldernhalle, which never looks more imposing than when half concealed in the mystery of shadows, across the busy Platz, now twinkling with countless lights, by the statue of Lewis the First, and in at the door of the old Conservatory itself.

December 18.

To-day came the *Probe* in the big hall for the concert next week. The regular Conservatory chorus has been enlarged by a number of new voices, some of which are shrill enough to pierce through the dome itself. I came home utterly exhausted, for we were kept singing and standing three hours, and never in the annals of conducting was there a more wretched rehearsal. For the first time I saw a new side of Stavenhagen; he literally raged, but instead of making himself ridiculous he was positively majestic. To be sure, he got very red in the face, and his blond, curly hair, through which he despairingly thrust his hands, was much awry, but he stamped about on his bit of platform so ferociously, shook his baton so threateningly, and shouted his commands in such sonorous German that I trembled in my American shoes.

We sang first Liszt's "Excelsior." Why is it that the most shrinking, retiring, and timid-appearing member of an orchestra is always the one to play the instruments of percussion? One can easily imagine a stout, muscular creature presiding at the kettledrums, but when we come to look for him we discover him at the end of the line of flutists, playing the piccolo. The eternal law of opposites is, I suppose, as applicable here as elsewhere. An unusually meek man was to manage the bells which play such an important part in this work, and he continually came in half a beat late. Stavenhagen glared at him darkly, tried him several times, and then gave it up as hopeless. The chorus attacks were frightful, and each part sang at its own sweet will.

The Brahms Requiem began more auspiciously, and as the beautiful first movement, which we really sang well, went on, the director's tense expression softened, and he relaxed into his usual easy beat, hand on hip. At the close, where the sopranos end with the *pianissimo* phrase, "*selig sind*" (blessed), and the tenors come in yet fainter after them, and the whole thing dies away as might the distant notes of a celestial choir, we were gratified to hear him murmur "*Sehr schön!*" He praised us, too, for the second movement.

Isn't it magnificent when the whole chorus sing in unison that grand, broad theme, "*Denn alles Fleisch ist wie Gras*" (Behold all flesh is as grass)? And then the tender melody, "*So seid nur geduldig*" (Therefore be patient), which follows! It nearly swept me off my feet. Let critics say what they will, I love the work, and think perhaps, after all, Mr. Huneker is right in saying that Brahms is the first composer since Beethoven to sound the note of the sublime.

We were just congratulating ourselves on getting through very creditably, when alas! we stumbled upon the pitfalls and snares of that most difficult of fugues, "*Der Gerechten Seelen*" (The righteous souls). There is a bit of it where the tempo is amazingly tricky, and I remember no place, even in Bach's B minor Mass, so difficult to sing well. The girl beside me, who had a high, shrill voice, insisted on coming in a measure too soon, and this repeated mistake set our director's nerves on edge.

"*Die Erste Sopran! Die Erste Sopran!*" (The first soprano!) he cried, shaking his baton at our corner. Over and over we sang the same bars, but never once perfectly. Finally he threw down his stick, and with a desperate "*Ach, Gott!*" put his hands over his ears.

The chord broke off abruptly. The orchestra, plainly very bored, carelessly examined their instruments. The other members of the chorus looked at us reproachfully. We looked anywhere we dared. The first sopranos were in disgrace.

After what seemed an interminable silence, in reality about half a minute, Stavenhagen picked up his baton and said calmly, sternly, his voice cutting the stillness, "We will go on."

Well, we got through somehow, but it was after eight o'clock when I ran down the snowy street back to the *pension*. The family were at supper and the anxious face of *Mütterchen* looked relieved as I opened the door.

"We thought you were lost, isn't it?" said the Herr Doktor, in what he considered unimpeachable English.

Fräulein Hartmann, looking charming in a light-blue gown which she had donned in honor of Lieutenant Blum, her aunt's guest that evening, jumped up and ran to meet me.

"I'm so glad you are here safe," said she. To her the idea of a girl being out alone after six o'clock was almost inconceivable.

"I myself was on the point of going in search of *gnädiges Fräulein*," said Lieutenant Blum, with a low bow, much rattling of sword, and that sneering smile which even his great black mustache fails to conceal.

"That was indeed kind of you, *Herr Leutnant*," I replied as sweetly as possible. "You really didn't think me lost, or kidnapped, or perchance murdered in cold blood, did you?" I added to *Mütterchen*, as I took my seat.

"I might have thought even such frightful things as those, had not our friend opposite insisted that you had been detained and that there was no need of 'putting up my umbrella till it rained,'" she answered.

I looked gratefully across the table at the Poet's Wife, who smiled understandingly back. Hers is one of those sunny, unselfish natures which, "when they have passed the door of Darkness through," leave the world a better place than they found it.

The serenity of perfect poise is such an enviable thing to possess! Alas, that it is so seldom found in people of a musical temperament! I can hardly imagine a placid Tschaikowsky or an unruffled Dvorák, can you?

Christmas Day.

Stille Nacht, heilige Nacht!

Alles schläft, einsamwacht,

Nur das traute hochheilige Paar,

Holder Knabe im lockigen Haar

Schlafe in himmlischer Ruh'.

Can you see us as we stood on Christmas Eve in the quaint dining-room singing together the old carol which has rung throughout Germany on this night for centuries gone by? We formed a strange congregation—all wanderers from different parts of the globe, for once united by the Christmas spirit. There were eleven of us in all,—the Baron and Baroness with Karl between them, their rosy, good-natured faces sober and reverential; Herr Doktor, standing near, his critical expression softened as, under the spell of the song, his thoughts turn to his Paris hearthstone; Frau von Waldfel, forgetting, in the meaning of the hour, to wonder what sort of goodies we were to have for dinner; Fräulein Hartmann, lost in a dream, at her side; the Poet and his sweet-faced wife, holding each other by the hand as they joined firmly in the refrain; Herr Martens, abandoning his student airs to add a tenor, and last—but best of all—*Mütterchen*. I sat at the piano to play the accompaniments, where I could see not only them, but catch a glimpse of the servants who stood together outside in the hall. They were all arrayed in their best. Georg, especially gorgeous in the splendor of a new livery with fully six dozen brass buttons, stood in the front row. Next him was the cook, resting her hand on the head of her little girl, who had been granted leave from the convent to attend this gala occasion. The other servants crowded together behind them. For this one evening in the year caste was forgotten, and the Baroness's strong soprano joined with the alto of her maid as they led the rest in the hymn each had sung from childhood.

All went well till we reached the second verse. Then I heard Herr Martens' voice tremble, then break, then cease altogether. Poor fellow! his family is scattered over two continents, and for him the word Home is associated only with a sense of forlornness and loss. Gretchen, our own little maid, but a year away from the Bavarian Highlands, hid her face on Therese's shoulder. I looked at *Mütterchen* bravely singing, but I knew in my heart that she was thinking of Home. The picture of those around the table across the sea flashed across me and I felt an odd tightening at my throat.

It was only for a moment—this shadow of sadness on us all. Then it suddenly vanished, for at the last note the Baron flung open the double doors of the salon and ah! what a bewildering, fascinating, wonderful tree was revealed! Karl and I exchanged glances with satisfied smiles. We were proud of our work. The hours of labor in the morning spent in tying on the varicolored balls, in hanging the tinsel favors, in arranging the silver shower had not been in vain. It was indeed a marvellous shower, delicate, fairy-like, falling from the very topmost bough, where stood the figure of the Christ-child with outstretched hands as if to bless those below.

For a moment we were breathless with admiration. Then "All for the presents together," shrieked Karl in glee, "*Eins, zwei, drei!*" and in we went.

Along the sides of the room ran tables covered with a white cloth and trimmed with evergreen. On these the gifts were laid, not done into parcels, but tastefully arranged. Each person had his own particular group, and over it hung a bough of green and a basket of cakes and candy. In one corner was a large table for the servants. *Mütterchen* and I could not help smiling to hear the flood of joyous exclamations on every side as we examined our presents. The German language seems to have an endless supply of adjectives expressive of delight. There are thousands of them, ranging from the sonorous *grossartig*, with the prolonged rolling of the *r*s, to that overwhelming one which has such a wealth of emphasis on the last syllable, *kol-os-sál!* When they are all, as it were, turned on together, the effect is torrential!

After we had looked at our gifts and admired those of every one else, and the servants, beaming with happiness, had shaken hands and expressed their thanks, we went into the dining-room. Of course there was a *Bowle* and we drank, standing, a toast to "Merry Christmas." Then we played a lot of games, which although childish afforded us much amusement. Lieutenant Blum, with mustache more marvellously twisted than ever, came in and joined us, and later Edith and Louise with a lieutenant of the Second Regiment appeared. Just before twelve we all set off for St. Michael's to attend the midnight mass.

The great cathedral was crowded when we entered, and we could only find places in the chancel on the left of the altar. Thus we had a good view down into the church itself, and by the flickering light on the pillars dimly discerned the vast crowd kneeling in the pews, blocking the aisles, and occupying every portion of available space. Beyond them and above hovered mysterious shadows. It was almost oppressively silent. Only the footsteps of those entering broke the intense stillness. The sound, dying away in weird echoes high up beneath the vaulted roof, made the silence which followed more absolute.

Suddenly the big bell on the Frauenkirche began to toll in wonderful, mighty throbs. At the same moment, from above among the shadows, floated down the sound of music—exquisite strains of Palestrina. The door on our left opened and a long line of priests entered, clad in magnificent robes of white and gold. We all fell on our knees in the semi-darkness, our eyes turned towards the high altar, which alone gleamed like a gorgeous jewel beneath the rays of a hundred tapers. The impressive service began.

Through hazy clouds of incense I gazed down on the kneeling, worshipping crowd, kneeling and worshipping just as thousands of other throngs were doing at that very hour, here in far-off Germany, in France, in Italy, and across the sea. The marvellous, beautiful meaning of it all stirred me. My mind turned back through the ages to that night in the dusky stable of Bethlehem. Surely it is the wonder of all wonders that one Life—one brief, mortal Life, lived among millions of other lives—now after the passing of centuries stands out as the sole link uniting all Christendom.

Lost in the beauty of the service with its lights and incense and music and gold-decked priests, it was with a start that I awakened as it were from a spell when the music ceased, and the priests had filed out through the arched door. The cathedral felt suddenly damp and chill, and shivering, I pulled my cloak around me.

"I didn't care for the organist's selection at all," said Polly critically, as we turned to go.

"We must walk as quickly as possible or we shall all be ill for a week with colds from sitting so long in this damp church," added Edith in her emphatic way.

But the Poet's Wife said nothing. She only looked at me with her deep, unfathomable eyes, and pressed my hand gently. Sometimes she reminds me of you, Cecilia. She is one of the few in the great world who Understand.

V

MERAN, *January 1, 1903.*

The Happiest of New Years to you, Cecilia! Have you ever been among the mountains in winter? Have you ever run away on a holiday to a quaint little town nestling in the valley, and wandering through narrow streets and climbing up snowy roads forgotten that such things as canons or double counterpoint exist? If not, Cecy *mia*, get out your hood and fur coat and start! But before you go, let me tell you that I have a deep-rooted conviction: namely, that you can find no more entrancing spot on the globe than Meran. For Meran, you must know, lies exclusively apart from the rest of the world, deep down in the valley of the Adige and jealously guarded on every side by high mountains, like a jewel in a casket. The mountains themselves, covered with snow from base to summit, are so magnificent and stirring that I call them Wagner mountains. And oh! the sunset on their frosty peaks, when all the white is changed to rose—it beggars description.

We left München on Christmas Day—just after my writing you. All the *pensionnaires* and servants came to the carriage and bade us good by with much hand-shaking and expressing every possible good wish for a pleasant journey, just as if we were to be gone a year instead of ten days. Can you imagine spending Christmas riding through the Brenner Pass? Let me tell you, too, there never can be anything more marvellous than this same Brenner Pass in winter. There has been a heavy storm for some days and it left the whole country half buried in a white cloak. Snow, snow everywhere, covering every mountain, stretch of valley, and hill! It is a grand sight. We were so enchanted with the scenery that we forgot to mourn the lack of holiday festivities. Then, too, we did have one important feature of the season, for it only needed a glance out of the windows to discover a Christmas tree. Indeed we were in the midst of a whole forest of them, only in place of tinsel and spangles we had the lovelier decoration of pure snow, and instead of brilliantly colored favors, from every branch hung pendants of flashing ice, which, like finely cut gems, reflected the sunlight in flashes of all the colors of the rainbow.

On the train who should chance to be in the next compartment but Miss B—— from California, one of the students at the Conservatory. We had a delightful chat over music. She is studying with Krause, and told me quite a little about him. She says he is very erratic in his teaching and never gives a lesson twice alike. Sometimes he paces up and down the room while the pupil is playing. Often he gazes abstractedly out of the window for fully a quarter of an hour, saying nothing. Again, he stands with his back to the stove, hands behind him, apparently listening; then suddenly darts out of the room and does not return for twenty minutes.

"When he teaches Beethoven it is a different story," she went on. "He likes to do that better than anything. He draws up a chair and sits close beside the pupil, following every note. The slightest mistake is not overlooked. It's a fearful ordeal!"

We changed cars at Bozen, for only a single branch road, winding through the picturesque valley of the Adige, connects Meran with civilization. On our arrival we found the heartiest of welcomes from our friends the S———s who were at the station. We drove at once to their home, which is called "Villa Pomona," and is situated on the hill overlooking the town. The servants greeted us at the gate, and the dogs came bounding out with enraptured barks. Turning into the path leading to the house I had my first good look at the villa. It is square, and constructed of yellowish stone. Between the windows are frescoes representing the goddess of plenty, the graces, etc. A terrace runs around it. It reminds one, in a way, of the Pompeian houses. Inside, it is no less charming, and oh! so delightfully American in its furnishings and arrangement! The only discord in the harmony are the German porcelain stoves, but one can't have everything and live in the heart of the Austrian Tyrol too.

We breakfast in the loveliest room upstairs. The windows command such an inspiring view that one almost forgets to eat. Below lies the valley itself with its one church spire and its mass of quaint, low yellow buildings huddled together; on the heights at the right rises an old, crumbling tower, the remnant of a once splendid castle; on the left stretches out the valley, and far away there in the distance, so far that the blue of the sky becomes misty, one sees the first spurs of the Dolomites which guard the gateway into Italy. On every side rise these majestic mountains of snow, whose peaks look as if cut out by a giant knife, and laid against the background of an intensely blue sky.

When we have finished breakfast we generally take a walk to town. Our objective point is the post-office, but we would accept almost any pretext to wander down the hill and join the crowd strolling in the sunshine on the Gisela Promenade. The Promenade lies across the river, for an impetuous little stream cuts the village into two sections. Accordingly, at the foot of the hill we cross the most picturesque of stone bridges and find ourselves at once on the broad walk, which, lined with fine old poplars, runs straight along the bank of the river. At eleven o'clock the walk is crowded. Meran is not only a fashionable resort in winter, but a favorite spot for invalids on account of the perfection of its climate. One sees them always on the Promenade at this time, walking slowly up and down, leaning back in wheel chairs, listening to the music of an excellent *Capelle*, as they call the orchestra, which plays here daily. If the weather happens to be cold, which is seldom the case, the music can be enjoyed in the luxurious Curhaus especially built for the purpose.

It was just by the band-stand, in the delightful sunshine of our second morning here, that I had the pleasure of meeting Carl Zerrahn. You remember the time when he was such a prominent conductor and musician in Boston, do you not? We had sat down to rest and hear the music when Mr. S—— pointed to the tall, commanding figure of an elderly man slowly approaching.

"Here comes Zerrahn," he said; "he is, alas, almost blind now, and cannot recognize any one except at close range."

A thrill of sadness swept over me, as I recalled him as the first conductor I ever saw, standing on the stage at the old Music Hall and sweeping the Handel and Haydn Society along in those great choruses of the "Messiah" and "Elijah." His hair is now snow white, and his walk feeble, but he stands as proudly erect as when he wielded the baton in the height of his success.

He did not perceive us approaching, although the members of the *Capelle*, who all knew him, watched us curiously. When we were within a few feet of him, we introduced ourselves as old friends whom he had, perhaps, by this time forgotten. It was charming to see his frank delight in meeting us again and in learning news of Boston, which he loves very dearly.

"I am staying with my son here," he said, "but I feel that Boston is my home, and I shall go back there in a year or so. I worked and lived and grew in Boston. It is to me what no other city is."

He asked about the Handel and Haydn Society, inquired about my musical studies and the Munich opera, and was so thoroughly kindly and interested in everything pertaining to his art that I could not but think of Victor Hugo's lines, "There are no wrinkles on the heart."

In the afternoon we go driving over some of these countless roads about Meran. It is like travelling through a magnificent picture gallery. The other day we went shopping. You never saw anything so fascinating as the stores. The principal ones are in the "*Lauben*," the quaintest of streets, whose sidewalks are built under arcades. When we enter, the girl in attendance always says "*Küss' die Hand*." The first time I heard this I frankly put out my hand to be kissed. A laugh from them all made me blushingly draw it back again. I learned that even here in this cool sequestered vale of the Adige people do not say what they mean. It seems the proper thing to murmur "*Küss' die Hand*," but no one but a servant would ever think of actually doing it. It is a sort of "take the will for the deed" arrangement.

The prettiest thing happened here this New Year's morning. We were all sitting in Mr. S——'s study hearing the latest American paper (two weeks old) read aloud, when there came a rap at the door. A moment later the gardener, his wife, and two little girls entered, dressed in their holiday clothes.

They all bowed solemnly. Then the parents withdrew to the background, the father nervously turning his cap around in his brown hands, while his wife, in true German fashion, held the bundle, a huge thing clumsily done up in white paper. The older of the two little girls, who could not have been more than five, shyly advanced. In a high, excited voice she recited a little poem about the New Year. Her sister, no less thrilled by the occasion, recited very rapidly two more verses about *Freude* (joy) and *Glück* (happiness). As a finale they together took the bundle and with the prettiest of courtesies handed it to Herr and Frau von S——, "with best wishes for a happy New Year and many thanks for their kindness." The S——s were much pleased and touched by this charming simplicity. The package proved to be a beautiful plant of azaleas, and the whole quartet were radiant with delight as we passed the gift among us and praised its beauty. They went away with many bows, looking, oh! so happy, and Mrs. S—— ordered an extra supply of beer for them in the kitchen.

That reminds me of a curious custom here. Did I tell you that a servant is engaged at so much a week *with* beer?[1] Mrs. S—— says the maids make a dreadful uproar if their beer is not forthcoming, and the cook insists on several bottles a day. I should think this might be detrimental to the cooking, but Mr. S—— assures me that it has quite the contrary effect, and the more beer she drinks the better she cooks.

This afternoon we took a long drive, returning through the town, so I had a fine chance to see the peasants in gala array. Near a wayside shrine (one finds them everywhere here) we came upon a crowd of young peasants sitting on the stone wall, or leaning lazily against it smoking meerschaum pipes. The splendor of their costumes was quite startling. Their funny little round hats, usually severely plain, were coquettishly decorated with bunches of yellow flowers fastened on the brim at the back. Their coats and trousers were of corduroy. Most noticeable of all were their waistcoats of scarlet or bright green.

"They seem to have very pronounced tastes," I remarked. "Isn't it odd that some of them choose red and the others choose green, as if they belonged to a college team?"

"There is method in their madness," answered Mr. S—— laughingly. "A much more serious matter than a question of taste is at stake. Let me inform you immediately, my dear young lady, that those whom you see before you in red waistcoats are married men, while those in green are bachelors and in the market, so to speak. It strikes me as not a half-bad idea. Surely a girl can't innocently fall in love with the wrong man here."

"Unless she is color-blind," I added.

It is time for supper, and as Mrs. S—— has promised us a real American meal I don't want to risk being a second behindhand. No one can realize what that means—a real American meal—unless one has been living for four months on a German *pension* diet. Why, after so many foreign menus, I feel like the poor soul who "near a thousand tables pined and wanted food." Yesterday we actually had muffins for breakfast. Think of that when one is living in a country where the mere hint of hot bread or ice water calls forth the remark, "I do not see why all you Americans don't die of indigestion."

I can't get it out of my head that the officer I met on the Promenade this morning was Lieutenant Blum. He passed by with a number of other officers and several showily dressed women, all talking and laughing loudly. It is quite possible that he might have come down here on leave, but hardly probable under the circumstances. I did not get a full look at his face. It was the swaggering walk and the little fat hand raised to salute a brother officer that made me start and look again. By that time he had almost passed. Nonsense! Probably this very minute he is at the *pension* accepting a cup of tea from Fräulein Hartmann's slender hands, while Frau von Waldfel from behind the urn regards him with admiring glances, for of course the Fräulein is not allowed to see him alone. That would be a frightful breach of etiquette. Well, I will let you know when I return. For her sake, I rather hope I was mistaken.

INNSBRUCK, *January 3*.

Yesterday we regretfully left Meran, but the memory of our delightful stay there will long haunt us, and we are living in hopes of another visit to this earthly paradise. We reached Innsbruck at three o'clock, and by four found ourselves here, in this most fascinating of houses—for, Cecilia, we are actually living, eating, sleeping in a castle, a real, *bona fide* castle, once the hunting lodge of the Emperor Maximilian. I see you start and your eyes glow. "A fig for music!" you say; "Let me live in your castle." Yes, you who so revel in mediævalism, to whom the glimpse of faded tapestries and dulled armor is as so much wine, would surely be in your element here.

How this former resort of knights and retainers sank to the materialistic, twentieth-century level of a *pension* I have not yet learned, nor cared to. All I know is that the grand old dining-room, hung with ancient portraits of the royal house, still remains; that the carved balconies with their worn railings overlooking the rushing stream of the Inn, the narrow winding corridors, the high diamond-paned windows, the picturesque terrace, the goblets, beakers, and trophies of the hunt are yet here—decaying relics of a brilliant past.

This morning I discovered the crowning feature beneath this most enchanting of roof-trees. Leaving *Mütterchen* to toast her feet by the fire, I went in search of a book in the library. In the many twistings and turnings of the corridors I lost my way. At length I found myself at the top of a short flight of steps, and thinking this was only another way to the library, I walked down them and along the hall. A worn door was at the end. I pushed it open and entered. For a moment the darkness of the place blinded me, coming as I had from the brightness of the outer house. Then I saw more clearly there were people, yes, actual, live people, kneeling on the stones and telling their beads within touch of my hand. No one noticed me as I stood by the door. As I looked about me I saw that I was in a chapel all of stone. Before me was an altar decorated garishly with paper flowers. The light of the sacrament burned dimly above, and cast a shadow on the rough crucifix hanging near. A few rays of sunlight sifting in through the high window at the farther end of the room sent a shattered shaft across the heads of the peasants, who, absorbed in prayer, made no movement save to slip their beads along their rosaries. The suddenness of the change, the sense of awe in coming upon this one room, this one place set aside as a shrine in the very midst of a busy household, was startling. I felt myself an intruder, and noiselessly slipped away.

Upon inquiry at luncheon I discovered that it is the regular custom on fête days for the people of the village to climb up the hill and attend mass where the ruler of their fathers was wont to worship. On a second visit I discovered that on the right, just after entering the chapel, is a tiny square room which at a first glance looks like a cell. In the rough stones of the wall a square hole is cut, and beneath it is a bench to kneel upon. This place was the private oratory of the Emperor, and here he used to attend mass, receiving the sacrament through the orifice in the stones.

Can you imagine anything more fascinating than living in a house where every nook and corner is alive with memories of the past? I could stay here for weeks, but vacation is over and we leave for Munich to-morrow.

January 11.

Here we are again in old München! Every one in the *pension* expressed him or herself as delighted to see us back, with all that cordiality which is one of the most charming characteristics of the German nature.

I began again my lessons with Thuille on Wednesday. I had sent him at Christmas a little remembrance, as is the custom here. Naturally I expected he would thank me, but I was hardly prepared for what followed. As at his "*Herein!*" I entered the smoke-wreathed studio, he tossed his cigarette into the waste-basket, jumped up from his desk, and with both hands extended came to meet me.

"*Ach! gnädiges Fräulein!*" he exclaimed, "you were so kind to remember me in that charming way." Then what do you think he did? He bent over my hand in the most dignified way and kissed it. I felt like an empress holding court, and blushed to the roots of my hair at the honor he had done me. I took my accustomed chair beside his at the piano, inwardly praying that it would not be my ill luck to push off to the floor any one of the dozens of cigarettes which always lie carelessly strewn about. Then I placed my fugue on the music rack. Whatever I bring, be it sonatina, invention, or merely a counterpoint exercise, Thuille daringly plays it out *forte*. This is so different from the way Mr. Chadwick does. He seldom if ever touches the piano when looking over work, but takes the sheet and leaning back in his chair "hears it in his head," marking the mistakes with a blue pencil. My fugue was pronounced *recht gut*, which made me very happy, for I had spent several hours over it. When Herr Professor had finished with my work he brought out a piece of music from the cabinet.

"Here is a thing which is worth your while to study," he said. It was Mozart's Serenade in B flat major for wind instruments, including the *corno di basetto* and the *contrafagotto*. If you want a task, try to play it from score at sight. Thuille rattled it off as though it were the simplest exercise. I could not repress a sigh when he had finished.

"*Ach Gott*, my child!" he exclaimed, smiling at my hopeless expression; "I don't expect you to play it now like that. Study the construction and the instrumentation. You will learn much from it."

As I rose to go I noticed a number of loose manuscript sheets on his desk.

"This is a new piece for orchestra I am doing," said he.

A page of full orchestra score always fascinates me. It's rather odd, when you stop to think of it, now isn't it, that all those little black dots with tails to them represent actual sounds of different instruments and that they together produce an harmonic whole? There is as much individuality in the writing of these dots as in handwriting. Thuille's notes are very small, distinct, and closely written. Professor Paine has a large, firm hand. Chadwick's notes appear as though hastily dashed off, although perfectly legible. I remember distinctly the day he showed me the score of his brilliant Symphonic Sketches. It looked interestingly complex, although, to tell the truth, what impressed me most were the original verses which preceded each sketch. They cleverly portray a definite mood, and are, as it were, the key to what follows. Never by any chance do these appear in the program book, so the listener is left to puzzle out for himself just what the composer means to convey.

I am to begin soon to study overture form, and Thuille asked me to bring Beethoven's overtures with me at my next lesson.

Later.

We are both much struck with the change in Fräulein Hartmann. She is much paler than she was before we went to Meran, and flushes nervously at the least excitement. *Mütterchen*, who has the misfortune to be next to Frau von Waldfel at table, inquired if her niece were ill.

"Indeed, no!" answered the Hungarian woman somewhat sharply. "What can you expect when a girl betrothed to an officer makes ready for a grand wedding in the spring? There is much to be done and dozens of gowns to be ordered. My niece is merely tired with the happiness of it all."

At that moment I caught Fräulein Hartmann exchanging a glance across the table with the Poet's Wife. In that one, quick flash I read many things, for the eyes of the former betokened genuine distress, while the reassuring look which met hers was that of a sympathizing friend. A second later the Poet's Wife was tactfully leading Frau von Waldfel to give her views on the new cooking-school, while Fräulein Hartmann abstractedly replied to the queries of a stout American woman who sat next her. This new arrival is merely here for a few days. She and her apologetic-appearing husband are "doing" Germany, Italy, and France complete in three weeks.

"I want ter know where those pictures of Reuben are. Baedeker stars 'em three times," said the stout traveller, turning to me.

I was longing to ask "Reuben who"? but *Mütterchen*, evidently sensing my temptation, pressed my foot under the table; so I merely said as politely as I could, "I think you mean the pictures in the old Pinakothek by Rubens," and gave them the directions to Barer-strasse. While they were commenting upon them, I wondered what could have happened during our absence to make Fräulein Hartmann and the Poet's Wife close friends. I wanted to ask if Lieutenant Blum had been at Meran, but intuitively I felt it best not to mention the subject. Here is indeed a romance to which I have found no key, as Omar would say.

The Conservatory is open again and everything is in full swing. In spite of the fact that I have very little opportunity to practise on the piano—because my work for Thuille requires the greater part of my time,—I enjoy the lessons immensely. When we read at sight I find them especially interesting. We have been playing some splendid things for two pianos, among them those lovely Schumann variations in D major. If you don't know them get them by all means. Yesterday we finished Brahms' symphony in E minor, with its vigorous *allegro giocoso*, and have begun Liszt's Symphonic Poems.

How everything helps everything else in music! The orchestra reveals its nuances twice as clearly when one is familiar with the actual material of a work, and then in composition it is absolutely necessary to have a broad field of literature from which to draw models and examples.

Poor Frau Bianci is in a terrible state over my pronunciation of German. "It will go in speaking," she says, "but, *ach Gott!* must be much finer for singing!" I managed to get Beethoven's "*Kennst du das Land?*" to suit her, but only after much toil for both of us. I repeated each phrase a dozen times after her before I was allowed to sing it. Truly, I feel very young and irresponsible. Don't talk about musical temperament and feeling to me! My one idea is to get the vowels open enough and to pronounce these fiendish umlauts in the approved fashion. I fell down most shamefully on Schubert's "Marguerite at the Spinning-Wheel." You know how wonderfully sad and beautiful that is. Bianci was quite pleased at my rendering of the first verse. Then I sang the second, where the music works up climactically and the words run,

"Sein hoher Gang, sein' edle Gestalt,

Seines Mundes Lächeln, seiner Augen Gewalt,

Und seiner Rede Zauberfluss,

Sein Händedruck, und ach, sein Kuss!"

At this point Frau Bianci broke off playing, and leaned back in her chair with a sigh. Then she said with cutting sweetness of tone, "The idea of this song is to make your audience cry, not to make them laugh. That word is *Lächeln, Lächeln, Lächeln!*"

I felt as though I had suddenly shrunk from Marguerite to a naughty child of five. Then a sense of rebellion stirred me. I wanted to tell her that I had not been born with a German throat, and that such things as umlauts were a disgrace to any language. However, I controlled myself and said nothing.

"I think you had better go into Hofregisseur Müller's class," she said. "It will be of great benefit to you. Please attend to-morrow at nine o'clock."

Very meekly I answered, "Yes, Frau Professor," as I picked up my music and went out, not having the faintest idea who Hofregisseur Müller was, nor what his sonorous title meant.

At nine the following day I was at the Conservatory. On the stairs I met Miss P——, a Philadelphia girl who is in my piano class. She explained to me that Herr Müller was the Regisseur, that is, the coach for acting at the opera house, and that his class was the *Aussprache*, or dramatic class, for the vocal students who were to sing in public. She herself is studying for opera and finds her work with him very beneficial.

"But I'm not going on the stage," said I, quite startled. "What does one have to do?"

Miss P—— laughed at my distressed expression. "Why, nothing but read before the class. Your pronunciation is corrected by Herr Müller. It is just as good as a German lesson," she said. "Oh, by the bye, don't mind if they laugh at you. They always laugh at foreigners."

With this parting shot as my encouragement, I went in. The room, on the upper floor just opposite the hall where we have the chorus rehearsals, is large and barnlike. A grand piano stands in dignified solitude in the centre, and at the end, near the green porcelain stove, is a long table around which the class sits. Herr Müller has his place at the head. He is an interesting type of man, very portly, with snow-white hair and mustache, and a pair of noticeably keen, speculative eyes. The appreciation of the humorous is strongly marked on his broad features.

"*Eine Amerikanerin!*" he said, smiling, as I came in. It is odd how quickly the people here detect our nationality. He motioned me to a chair, then slowly drew a large watch from his pocket and laid it on the table before him.

"Well, Fräulein, what have you?" he inquired of the first girl on his left, who promptly handed him the "Bride of Messina" and going to the farther end of the room began to recite shrilly a passage by heart. At every line the Herr Regisseur would thunder forth criticisms in his great, vibrant voice. When her turn, which lasted five minutes, was past, he called on the next girl, a soft-voiced, shrinking creature in a low-necked blouse. She murmured haltingly that she had "*Das Veilchen*" (The Violet). "*Ach! Das Veilchen!*" lisped he, with his head on one side, in the same tremulous tones. The imitation was such a capital one that we all laughed. In the bare room the effect was that of a hilarious whoop. I began to see what was in store for me. After a few wretched moments I determined to take the whole affair as a joke. There were nine girls to be called on before it came my turn, but in what seemed an incredibly short space of time they had all finished and Herr Müller was calling my name.

"Recite one verse very slowly," said he.

"*Meine Ruhe ist hin*" (My rest is o'er), I began bravely, feeling how poignantly applicable the line was to my present situation. Throughout my recital I could plainly hear titterings from the girls, but I kept my eyes firmly fixed on the picture of Beethoven over the door. When I had finished, Herr Regisseur laid the book down on the table, leaned back in his chair, and laughed. The whole class joined with him. Not to be outdone, I laughed too, albeit somewhat weakly.

"Now much louder and slower, *Fräulein aus Amerika*," he said. "Repeat after me, '*Meine Ruhe ist hin.*'"

It was the same thing that I had tried with Frau Bianci, only now I enunciated every syllable with painful effort, my voice pitched to *fortissimo*.

"Not bad," said he, when I had finished, although his eyes twinkled. "Learn another verse for next time."

We all went over to the Gärtner Platz Theatre last week to see "The Geisha." The little opera house is very cosy, but oh! how strange "The Geisha" sounded in its new word-clothes! From a musical standpoint it was delightfully given, but to my mind the Germans have not snap enough to produce light opera well. We have seen two or three things there, among them Strauss' charming *Fledermaus*, and have invariably remarked the same thing. The chorus sang excellently, but were selected with absolutely no eye for beauty or grace. And how the Amazons did wear their armor! They reminded me more of tired waitresses after a hard day's work than the spirited war-maidens they were supposed to represent. Sparkle, vivacity, delicacy,—all these elements which make light opera what it should be,—were lacking. I am convinced that God created the Germans for grand opera and that in the captivating froth of operettas they are distinctly out of their element. One wishes he might look into the music of the future and see how the school of the versatile American will eventually evolve; whether it will be individually characteristic, or blindly content to follow the path laid down by its forerunners across the sea.

There is splendid skating now in the *Englischer Garten*. Last Saturday after lessons six of us met at the *Sieges Thor* with our skates. The ice on the *Grosse Hesselohe*, the pond at the upper end of the garden, was in excellent condition. At the farther end of it the International Hockey Team, composed of men from the University of Munich and the Polytechnic, was having a match with some strangers. The Germans skate very well and seem devoted to the sport. This seems rather odd to me, as they do not as a rule care for outdoor exercise except walking. Golf is unknown as yet, and although they have a game which they call football, it would hardly be recognized by that name in our country.

We had a delightful afternoon and came back ravenous for supper.

Friday.

I haven't yet told you what a time I had to get the candy S—— sent. It was the day after your bountiful Christmas box came. By the bye, I trust you have received our acknowledgment of it by this time, and I want to tell you now that the plum pudding was not hurt a particle. The cook steamed it, and we invited all the *pensionnaires* to share it with us at dinner. If you could have but heard their compliments, you or your cook would certainly have blushed with pride. Why, even Frau von Waldfel confessed that, after all, people did have something good to eat in America, a fact she had never formerly believed. But about the candy.

In my morning's mail I found a *Legitimations-Karte*. Doesn't that sound imposing, as though I had graduated with honors from some academy? It really is nothing more than a statement that a package lies in the custom-house waiting to be called for. The office itself is in a large room like a hall, and full of all sorts of bundles, boxes, and burlap bags, which look like the accumulation of years. The blue-bloused *Dienstmann* behind the counter found my box for me and cut the string, for which I, of course, gave him a tip. (You know nothing is free in Germany. We have to pay even for our programs at the theatre or opera.[2])

Having concluded this first matter, I walked down a corridor and into the room on the right. Here I took my place at the end of a long line of people. It was certainly twenty minutes before I reached the scales, for all the packages are weighed, you know. With impressive dignity the burly man in charge leisurely weighed my box, recorded the number, and directed me into yet another room.

Accordingly I made my way to the desk where duties are registered. Here I waited again in line for some time. After all this red tape I fancied I should have to pay at least six marks, but when my turn came I found that only forty-five pfennigs were required before I could make my escape. As I began tying my box together yet another of these persistent officers accosted me.

"Your number," said he, as if I were a freshman taking an entrance examination. I stared at him, then recalled the red figures on my package.

"Two hundred and two," I said.

"You must step here," he announced authoritatively.

I was so tired of stepping this way and that, that my first impulse was to refuse, but for fear that this might mean the sacrifice of my real American candy, I followed him meekly into the next room, where he solemnly scribbled something in a big black book. Then, with a flourish which shook the gold fringe of his uniform, he handed me a paper.

"That is all," he said.

"All?" I asked. Now that escape seemed so near I doubted its possibility.

"That is all," he repeated, with a low bow. I turned on my heel and never slackened my pace till I was at the door of the *pension*. By this ridiculous proceeding I had lost just two hours on my counterpoint. The candy, however, is wonderful! I never tasted anything more refreshing. Certainly, Germany is no place for candy—nor for doing things quickly, either.

On the fifteenth came the first production in Germany of the French opera *Messidor* before a crowded audience at the opera house. The libretto is by Zola and the music by Bruneau. The work is typical of its school, especially in the orchestration. As in some of Massenet's pieces, the trombones burst forth every few minutes, as if to say, "Don't fancy for a moment, kind public, that we have gone out for a glass of beer. We never miss but a few bars." The so-called symphonic *Legende vom Golde*, a symbolic pantomime, if I may so call it, which opens the third act, struck me as unutterably tawdry, but the last scene had a perfectly charming setting, and the climax was very effective. At the final curtain the composer was called out several times, but the opinion of the audience seemed to be divided, for although the applause was plentiful, continued hissing from the opponents of the French school was distinctly audible. Bruneau is tall and slight, with black pointed beard and waxed mustache. He responded in several constrained little bows, as though charmed with the applause, and as if utterly unconscious of any less complimentary sounds.

We are hearing much talk of balls and frivolity, for the carnival is just beginning. Already the Baron is planning to make up a large party for something, and of course I shall write you all about it. Louise and Edith are coming over to do ear-training to-night at eight, and it is already time for supper, so this must end my letter for to-day. All good wishes for you.

M.

Do you know the "Beethoven-Lied" by Cornelius? The greater part of it is composed of the principal theme of the first movement of the Eroica Symphony. We sang it in the chorus hour on Thursday. I should think it might be a splendid thing for your club to work at.

VI

February 4.

Du liebes Cecilchen:—

I'd give every pfennig in my possession to walk into your study to-day and take you by surprise. In fact, I have stopped in the very midst of my orchestration lesson to tell you so. My chord of the seventh is unresolved, my flutes and oboes are hanging in midair, and my horns are blowing away on the fifth, all because a wave of the Indescribable swept over me, and I simply had to throw down my pencil and talk to you!

The preliminary symptoms of this abominable Something appeared this morning when my mail failed to arrive. Then after three hours' hard work on a new fugue-subject, I came to the conclusion that what I had written was absolutely worthless, and thrust it in the waste-paper basket. In the afternoon no letters came, but several newspapers, whose essential feature consisted in describing varied and brilliant festivities at home. I could not repress a sigh as I read. Finally Georg came bowing in with the announcement that the opera for the evening had been changed and *Der Freischütz* substituted for "Lohengrin." I felt like throwing my ink-well at the Obelisk, running down to the booking office in Promenade-Platz, and engaging a passage to America on the spot.

Not that I was really angry with the Obelisk, for I have but one dearer friend in all Munich, and that is the Fountain. The latter, however, no longer sings as I pass. It has, as it were, retired for the season, and a hideous paling of gray boards hides it completely from view. Such is the inartistic effect of winter. I can't tell you how much I miss its ever sympathetic, ever beautiful voice. Indeed, so barren and desolate is the upper end of the Platz, that I changed my route of walking and thus came to make the acquaintance of the Obelisk. Not only do I pass by daily, but whenever I look out of my window I can see in the distance its slender, black shaft sharply outlined against the sky. Strange, is it not, with what a keenly human note inanimate things sometimes appeal to us? Just as I hear and love the Voice in the Fountain, so I draw a feeling of protection from this towering creation of stone, as though a kindly sentinel were standing guard over me and mine.

Since my mood to-day is gray in color, I am going to tell you of the gayest thing which has happened since I wrote, namely, a gorgeous masked ball, for you know it is carnival season now and frivolity reigns supreme. I have been working so constantly lately—for my long lessons with Thuille and the work at the school take practically every moment of my time—that the ball seemed like an extraordinary piece of dissipation. Therefore I was quite excited as I joined the party of *pensionnaires* in the salon on Tuesday evening. What a cosmopolitan lot we were! The curious jumble of German, French, Italian, and English was laughable. The stout American and her pocket-edition of a husband have departed and given place to two Italian women who converse equally well in three languages. The Poet's Wife always speaks perfect French with Herr Doktor, which won his heart long ago. Of course we were all chatting of the frolic to come as we clambered into the droschkies awaiting us at the door. The ball, it seems, was given under the auspices of the press. The Baron had obtained invitations for us through a member of the *Jugend* staff. (The *Jugend* is that very artistic periodical which you have perhaps seen.) There were so many of us that a box had been engaged, for the affair was held at one of the theatres.

Every one who attended was obliged to wear a costume representing some feature pertaining to the woods, and it required no little thought to design something original and effective. Fräulein Hartmann and I had decided to go as flowers, and *Mütterchen* and the Poet's Wife put their heads together and created a Rose gown and a Violet gown. Frau von Waldfel was so agitated over her own costume that she quite forgot to criticise ours. She had chosen to represent a bee, and had arrayed herself in black netting. On her head was a crown of black and yellow, and from her shoulders hung, or should have hung, a pair of gauze wings. But something went wrong, and the wings, instead of suggesting airy flittings through space, drooped at a curious angle and gave the impression that they were not mates. However, her distress was mitigated by the Baroness, who declared that the costume was "wonderfully becoming," and as soon as she arrived she forgot to worry about her wings in the excitement of the ball itself.

What a fascinating sight burst upon us as we stepped inside the ballroom! The whole place was alive with a dancing crowd of fairies, gnomes, flowers, butterflies, and dryads, who flitted past in a bewildering whirl of ever changing color. All the women wore little black masks, which gave them a most coquettish appearance. The men were not masked, but their costumes were fully as artistic. As I watched the glittering throng moving to the strains of a fascinating waltz which came floating out from behind a grove of evergreens on the stage, I could easily fancy I was in fairyland.

Just as we were about to cross the hall Fräulein Hartmann caught me by the arm.

"I've torn my gown," she said in a hurried, excited manner, as she held up the ragged ruffle on the edge of her train. "I must go to the dressing-room and fix it. Will you tell my aunt? And oh! please say it may take twenty minutes or—or a half-hour."

I looked at her in surprise. Her cheeks were flushed brilliantly, and I would have given much to have seen the expression of her eyes, which her mask half hid.

"Why, if you would let me help you——" I began, but she interrupted, pressing my arm tighter.

"Let me go alone, please, *kleine Amerikanerin*." Her voice was pleading and oddly intense. "It's only such a short time—and, believe me, there is nothing wrong, *really*. I shall thank you always."

Before I had an opportunity to reply she had slipped away in the crowd. To say I was amazed were to put it mildly. I was dumfounded. Two points alone seemed clear in my mind: first, that Fräulein Hartmann had no idea of spending a half-hour in sewing on a few inches of ruffle; second, that whatever her motive for remaining away might be, it was "nothing wrong"; her frank, sweet nature utterly forbade such an idea.

Rather troubled, I caught up quickly with the others of the party and entered the box to find Lieutenant Blum and Lieutenant Linder waiting. They looked surprised at seeing me alone, and I hastily explained the situation. Lieutenant Linder then suggested that we three take a stroll about the hall, and we started off, I talking very rapidly, in the hope of turning their attention from the Fräulein's continued absence. I would not have been a woman had I not myself been a bit curious about her. We made a tour of the room and at length came to the head of a flight of stairs. I declared that I was dying of curiosity to discover what lay at the foot, so we descended and found ourselves in the very midst of a forest. On every side extended paths lined with trees whose branches met above in arches. At the end of one of the paths we saw a log hut. Above, through interlaced branches, shone a silver moon. I could not help exclaiming at the beauty of the illusion.

There were countless little arbors and retreats where couples were sitting out dances. We had just started to turn down the path to the right, when I caught sight of a rose-colored dress in one of these arbors. A step farther and I saw that the girl leaning against the bench was Fräulein Hartmann. Her head was thrown back in a characteristic attitude and her lips were parted, as though eagerly listening to the words of her companion. He—for of course it was a man—was a broad-shouldered fellow, with a smooth face and a sword-cut on his forehead. Bending forward, he looked up intently into the face of the girl, talking very earnestly, very rapidly, as if pleading a case under pressure of time.

Quick as a flash I wheeled about and faced the others, for the path was only broad enough for us to proceed in single file. I declared this walk stupid; the hut was the only thing really worth seeing; whereupon my bodyguard, although laughing at the capriciousness of my sex, obediently followed. How long I lingered about that wretched hut I can't say. At last, when every pretext was gone, I made my way back again upstairs. What a sigh of relief I gave when we reached the box, for there sat Fräulein Hartmann, smiling in her sweet, plaintive fashion, and talking to her aunt and Herr Doktor with the utmost self-possession. A moment later we had whirled away among the dancers, and I did not have an opportunity to exchange a word with her alone.

At twelve o'clock the orchestra stopped playing for an hour and supper was served. Half of the people had been eating and drinking the entire evening, for tables had been spread in the boxes from the opening of the ball. This did not, however, seem to make any difference in the keenness of their appetites now. We had a very jolly time in our box, for beside the *pensionnaires* were several Americans. Among them were Mr. and Mrs. Albert Sterner. You are doubtless familiar with the delightful work of Mr. Sterner. He has won considerable reputation, especially for his illustrations. Both he and his wife added much merriment to the party, for they are very entertaining. The ball began again at one, but no one thought of going home till four o'clock. We left Lieutenant Linder still dancing.

"This lasts till five," he explained, as he took us to our carriage. "I shall get a cup of coffee at the restaurant, change to my uniform, and be ready for *Dienst* (service) at six. I really haven't time to go to bed."

I captured two very pretty souvenirs of the occasion, one of which you shall have to decorate your den. Every one who went down on the floor wore a favor made of blue ribbon, fastened with a gold head of Folly. Lieutenant Linder and Herr Martens both presented me with theirs, and in spite of acquiring a habit for greediness, I smilingly accepted both, with a thought for you. They will look extremely well tacked to an American wall.

I did so wish for a word with Fräulein, but she drove home alone with her aunt. As I wrote you, I only see her at table, and so any conversation of a confidential character is out of the question. She is not a girl to practise deception, unless forced by circumstances, hence I fancy that there is something of a serious nature behind her action. Evidently the handsome young man with the sword-cut is the key to the mystery! Very likely she is in love with him, instead of with that disagreeable Blum. Were she an American girl it would not take her long to throw over the uniform and marry the man she loves; as it is, with her family and *an officer* weighing the balance on the opposite side of the scales, I fear the student's chances are not the most favorable.

After Supper.

At my last lesson Thuille informed me that he and Tasso were going hunting on Saturday. Would I pardon him if he gave me my lesson in his hunting costume? Accordingly to-day he appeared in a wonderful green shirt striped with white, and open at the neck. His jacket, short trousers and gaiters were of some rough cloth, and the effect was decidedly unprofessional.

The train left directly after the lesson, and Tasso was evidently quite alive to the fact, for instead of sleeping under the desk as he usually does, he roamed about restlessly during the entire hour, and finally became so importunate that his master unceremoniously put him out. I had taken in a practice piece scored for wood-wind and horn, including bass clarinet and contra-fagott. The ideas on which I had written the part for bass clarinet were suggested by that bit for the instrument in the third act of "Siegfried" where Brünnhilde is wakened by the all-powerful kiss. Unfortunately my result was not what might have been called an unqualified success. In one measure I had put a rest at the second beat, after writing two notes. This immediately attracted Thuille's attention.

"Why, you've left him hanging in the air! Poor fellow, he's hanging in the air between heaven and earth!" he said laughing, but not unkindly. I thought I ought to laugh too, so I joined in, nervously. It is queer how much more humorously these things strike one after a lesson than at the time they actually happen.

"This is the way he would have to play that," continued the professor. He puckered up his mouth, held his fingers exactly as the player would, squinted at my score with his head on one side, and blew two notes, "Poom! Poom!" Then he took the imaginary instrument suddenly away while his mouth seemed to be forming the same tone. He looked so funny that this time I could not help laughing heartily, and I saw my mistake at once.

Later we came to a horn passage, and in place of the mildly flowing chords in half-notes which I had written he substituted eighth-note phrases. "I thought that would be too fast," said I, in self-defence.

"Study modern scores!" he exclaimed. "Study modern horn parts! But don't forget the classics either; and never study Schumann or Brahms for orchestral writing. They were both poor scorers."

I sometimes wish he employed similes in his explanations; they have such a way of sticking in my head and making me remember. I recall now an especially vivid one which Chadwick once made to his orchestral class: "Here you have your instruments of the orchestra just like so many colors on a palette," he said. "You combine different ones just as you mix your colors, to obtain a desired effect. Your task is to make a complete, finished picture.

Choose your subject and go ahead, but take care to select your materials wisely."

If you remember, Professor John K. Paine has also a fondness for illustrating his point in this manner, only he chooses literature instead of art as the source from which to draw his comparisons. I can see us now sitting side by side in that dingy little room in Vaughan House before the new music room existed, taking notes on his lectures, and can hear him saying, "Beethoven is the Shakespeare of music." Do you remember the day when Miss R—— brought her dog into the class, and Professor Paine, after peering at it mildly over his glasses from his seat behind the table, made some witty remark about the increased interest in his lectures which now drew the very beasts to hear him? And later, how kindly but firmly he insisted that Miss R—— leave her pet at home hereafter, inasmuch as he had already punctuated his paper on Haydn, and he did not consider the assistance of the dog, who broke in every now and then with sharp barks, at all necessary.

As soon as the lesson was over I hurried home, for *Mütterchen* and I had seats for the *Zauberflöte* that evening. We had an early supper in our rooms, for the opera began at half-past six. I had not heard a Mozart opera since last September, when the Mozart-cycle was held in the Residenz Theatre. Then I enjoyed *Cosi fan tutte*, with Fritzi Scheff as Despina. The Residenz Theatre is an ideal place to hear Mozart. It is only large enough to seat eight hundred persons, and the orchestra sounds most effective. The Hof Theatre is too large for the production of Mozart's operas. After one act of the *Zauberflöte* I began to find the orchestra thin and somewhat monotonous. When the music is really so beautiful, it seems a pity not to give it under the best conditions.

Fräulein Hartmann and her aunt sat just across from us in the balcony. I hoped that we might all walk home together, but when we met at the door afterwards there was Lieutenant Blum, important and self-satisfied, waiting to escort them.

Good night now, my dear.

Fasching-Dienstag (Shrove Tuesday).

München gone mad! München with dignity thrown to the winds and cavorting in the dress of a clown! München laughing, dancing, fairly shrieking with pure glee! The misty atmosphere through which one always views the distant majesty of the Maximileum as one looks down Maximilianstrasse is curiously filled with a new sort of snowflake, a tiny, square atom which may be red or green or the most vivid of yellows. The sidewalks are packed with a half-crazed throng, some in vari-colored costumes, others in street dress, but all pelting one another with confetti, while the street itself is crowded with slow-moving lines of carriages whose occupants join no less wildly in the fun. And all this because it is the last day of the carnival.

My first glimpse of the frolic to come was afforded me on Saturday. I was deep in the midst of a canonic imitation when there came a knock on the door and in burst Karl, radiant, his cheeks aglow with excitement. He was dressed in a wonderful costume, which consisted of a loose white shirt with black silk pompons down the front, white trousers, a gigantic white ruff about the neck and a high pointed hat.

"*Bin ich nicht nett, gnädiges Fräulein?*" (Am I not fine?) he cried, kissing my hand with mock deference and prancing about the study. "Just wait till you see me to-morrow! Then I am to have a grand mustache and all kinds of red and green designs painted on my cheeks!"

He grinned with delight at the thought of these cannibalistic decorations, which, however, struck me as more appropriate for a circus than a Sunday promenade.

To-day *Mütterchen*, the Baroness, Herr Martens, and I took a carriage before the house at two o'clock. One's first carnival is not a thing to be taken calmly and I was all excitement, staring to right and left, and craning my neck in my endeavor not to miss anything. On every corner we passed stood old women and men with little pushcarts full of bright-colored bags of confetti or baskets of *Luft-Schlangen* (long paper streamers done up in small rolls, to be thrown through the air like those we have at the Harvard Class Day exercises around the statue). For ten pfennigs (two and one-half cents) one could obtain a generous supply, and following the Baroness' suggestion, we stocked the carriage well.

We found the streets already so crowded that we were forced to proceed very slowly towards Max-Joseph-Platz. Just as we reached the post-office a horn blew sharply, policemen hurriedly pushed back the crowd, and the First and Second Cavalry regiment officers came galloping by us and on down the street between the two long lines of carriages. Their appearance was most grotesque. Dressed as clowns, in suits of black or white, their painted faces made them all look alike. With snapping whips they urged on their horses at full speed. The excited animals seemed to enjoy the fun as much as their riders, and shook their gayly ribboned manes proudly.

Hardly had we started again, for our carriage had come to a halt to let them pass, when I heard a familiar voice cry, "Hola!" and as I turned to see who was shouting, a handful of confetti was thrown straight in my face. For a moment I was angry, for the sensation of eyes and mouth suddenly full of paper is not conducive to amiability. Then, realizing the absurdity of losing my temper at such a time, I dived my hand into a bag to retaliate on my antagonist. Before I could discover him another shot landed in the back of my neck and over my hat a *Luft-Schlange* came floating.

"Caught you that time, *gnädiges Fräulein*," said a voice, and I met the laughing glance of Karl, who jumped on the step of our carriage and rode along with us. His white costume was sadly soiled, but he had fulfilled all his promises as to the horrible wonder of a painted mustache and streaked cheeks. A North American Indian could not have improved on him.

"I've ridden up and down five times already," he said, as he jumped off to pay a similar visit to some friends just across.

"There's Lou and the girls," I cried, catching sight of a carriage in the opposite line coming up the street as we went down. Having learned my lesson I was not slow to put it in practice, for standing up in the carriage I pelted them mercilessly, Herr Martens supplying me with a fresh bag every time I needed one, and the Baroness joining enthusiastically in the attack.

It was not a one-sided battle, for the girls were quick to return our shots, and the aim of the little Italian count who was with them was excellent. You should have seen our carriage when they were finally out of range. The floor, up to our shoe-tops, was filled with confetti; our jackets were covered with it, and from the shoulders of the driver, from our hats, from the sides of the carriage hung countless brilliant streamers.

At the big statue we turned and came back. When we finally succeeded in reaching the post-office we found a most exciting thing taking place. A company of clowns on horseback, whom we recognized as the cavalry officers who had earlier passed us, were forming in line at the farther end of the Platz. Suddenly they set off with brisk canter, swung around the statue of Max Joseph, and dashed at full speed up the high flight of stairs leading to the opera house! They came back rushing down the driveway. The horses were almost beside themselves with excitement, for their officers leaning far forward, brandished their whips, dug in their spurs, and urged on the beasts by frantic shouts and exclamations, while the crowd of onlookers cheered wildly. It was a thrilling sight, and I watched them breathlessly. I could not help feeling that at any moment one of these half-crazed creatures, now flecked with foam, might lose his balance and fall backwards down the steps crushing his rider beneath, and so I gave a relieved sigh as I saw the men at last dismount, give their quivering steeds to an orderly, and adjourn to the café opposite. Just then the Baron and Herr Doktor, who were walking, came up to our carriage.

"We'll take you into the café for a moment," said the Baron. "It is apt to grow rather rough there later, but you must get a glimpse of another side of the carnival."

Accordingly, well barricaded by the gentlemen, we quietly entered the café and took the only vacant table which stood in a retired corner. Here again the officers had undisputed possession of the place. They were laughing, dancing and singing in a boisterous though not at all in an offensive fashion. Meanwhile an orchestra in the centre of the room played some lively music.

"Your selection pleaseth me but poorly," declaimed a tall fellow with a blue ruff about his neck, as he tapped on the shoulder of the director. "Why not soothe our ears with a ditty akin to this?" whistling one of the popular student airs. He seized the baton and mounted the platform, rapping sharply on the rack. The players, entering into the spirit of the thing, followed him perfectly. This was not so simple a matter as it sounds, for he conducted with a ridiculous exaggeration of all the mannerism, gestures and poses of Weingartner. It was very cleverly done and set every one into roars of laughter, especially when the fellow insisted on a *pianissimo* passage. Then he would tilt back his head, wave his left hand with that curious droop of the finger-tips so characteristic of the great conductor, and nonchalantly beat time with his stick at an angle directed towards heaven.

No sooner had he finished and returned with low bows of mock modesty to his place, than an officer in the corner jumped on top of a table and, stein in hand, began singing. The crowd, who had gathered around him, joined in the refrain, clinking their mugs together, for of course every one was drinking beer—*ça va sans dire*. If an officer chanced to be without any, he made his way to a table where some onlookers were sitting, and with a courteous "beg pardon," and a graceful raising of the pointed cap, helped himself to the largest stein from under the very nose of its owner, and walked serenely off. No one seemed to mind this, the original possessor of the beer least of all, for he laughed heartily, and ordered the waiter to bring him a fresh supply. The established rule of the carnival is to take everything in the greatest good humor and let the spirit of fun prevail.

"To your very good health! May you live long, be prosperous, and see many carnivals!" said another fellow as he helped himself to a stranger's wine and raised the glass to his lips.

"That's Count von E——," said the Baroness in a whisper, as he set down the glass, bowing gravely. "I should know his peculiar walk anywhere."

"It was certainly most interesting," said I, as after watching the frolic for half an hour we walked out into Perusia-strasse.

"You don't have anything half as jolly in America, do you?" said Herr Martens, with a tone of superiority in his voice. Whenever any one addresses me with that inflection my spread-eagleism is aroused. I immediately began to dilate on America and the American. This time I chose as my theme

"Fourth of July," which of all our celebrations seemed nearest akin to this, and my glowing description of the manifold features of Independence Day caused the carnival to seem like a children's festival.

Did I write you that the Americans in the *pension* opposite were to give a St. Valentine's party? Owing to illness it was postponed to the evening of *Fasching Dienstag*. Accordingly we finished our day by a dance and general frolic with the girls, which was one of the jolliest things I have been to this year. This letter is so full of frivolity that to tell you of my doings in a musical way seems most incongruous, so I will save all such items for my next.

As ever, dear Cecy,

M.

VII

March 3, 10.30 P. M.

I have just returned from the *Moderner Abend* at the Kaim Saal, and am so excited that to go calmly to bed and to sleep is an impossibility. I don't know when I have enjoyed anything as much. The concert, as you may have judged by the name, was made up of compositions by living composers. Stavenhagen arranged it and all the numbers but one were played for the first time. Here is the program:

1.	Singspiel Overture	Edgar Istel.
	First time!	
2.	*Ein Zweigespräch*, Tone-poem.	Max Schillings.
	(For solo violin, solo 'cello, and small orchestra.)	
	[Richard Rettich—Heinrich Warnke.]	
	First time!	
3.	Scene and Monologue of Lukas from the Opera *Der Conegidor*	Hugo Wolf.
	[Anton Dressler.]	
	First time!	
4.	*Klavierkonzert* (op. 6) in B flat minor	Felix vom Rath.
	[Anna Langenhan-Hirzel.]	
5.	III. Act of *Gugeline*	Ludwig Thuille.
	[Gugeline, Agnes Stavenhagen. The Prince, Franz Bergen.]	
	First time!	

The names in brackets are those of the soloists. For some reason or other the order was altered. Thuille's piece and Hugo Wolf's changed places. Edgar Istel, who conducted his own overture, is a tall, broad-shouldered, fine-looking young fellow, and a pupil of Thuille. I am in doubt as to his nationality for he certainly looks too well groomed for a German. The Schillings piece was a lovely, sustained thing. That man certainly knows how to write for the 'cello! We heard his opera *Ingwelde* last week, and remarked the same thing then. The third number was, however, *the* number of the evening. I wish I could describe to you the enchanting beauty of this music from *Gugeline*—its delicacy, freshness, and tenderness. And yet withal there is no semblance of insipidity about it, for in spite of the dominance of fanciful, graceful motifs the music every now and then assumes a more passionate tinge, as though an undercurrent of deeper feeling flowed beneath its charming surface. Agnes Stavenhagen, the wife of the director, sang with great niceness. Thuille has a trick of ending a phrase by a jump to a high *pianissimo* note, and she rendered this most effectively.

Prejudiced as I naturally was in favor of my Maestro, I was not alone in my enthusiasm, for at the close of the piece the audience burst into a storm of applause, cheering, stamping, and crying "Bravo! Bravo!" "Thuille! Thuille!" The whole house rose as one person. Thuille, who had been sitting about eight rows back, at length came forward. He did not mount the stage, but remained below the conductor's stand, bowing and smiling in the delightful, unaffected fashion peculiar to him. Again and again he was recalled, the audience remaining standing and applauding. Clearly, aside from his musical ability, he is a great favorite in Munich. When the tempest had at last subsided and we had settled back into our places, Frau Langenhan-Hirzel appeared to play the concerto of vom Rath. Her entrance was the signal for a fresh outburst of applause, and there was no more enthusiastic group in the hall than ours in the east corner, for Polly, Edith, and Louise are all her pupils and loyally adore her. "Frau Langenhan," as they generally call her, looked very young as she took her place at the piano. She is slight, and her short black hair curls roguishly about her head, while a pair of dark, innocent eyes give her an almost childlike appearance. But however youthful she may seem, she plays with a mastery and force unusual in a woman. Lescheticsky is proud of her I hear, and one can readily see why. The concerto itself is most brilliant and was originally composed and dedicated to her. Long and prolonged applause followed its close. Frau Langenhan-Hirzel bowed repeatedly, and at length vom Rath came forward and joined her. He is tall, with extremely light hair. In spite of his dignified bearing he was blushing up to his ears with embarrassment, and looked greatly relieved to sit down.

As for the last number, we had forgotten all about it, for we started impetuously off to the green room. When we entered, there was the little pianist calmly smoking a cigarette and carelessly shaking her black curls from to time with a characteristic movement of the head. The girls rushed enthusiastically up to her. After the first eager words of congratulation they presented me, and she was most cordial in her greeting as she turned and shook hands, holding her cigarette in her fingers. Quite a number of the German women smoke and she does so constantly, in fact even when giving lessons, which goes ahead of Thuille.

But my head all the time was full of *Gugeline*—how could one forget it?—and I looked about for Thuille. He was talking to Stavenhagen in the corner, with his back towards me. A moment later he turned, and as I went forward with outstretched hand he met me half way. The beauty of his music had so intensely moved me, that I grew excited when I endeavored to congratulate him, and my German flew away as if on wings. I could only murmur stupidly something about "*wunderschön*" (very beautiful) and "*entzückend*" (charming), the sole adjectives I could at the moment recall. Perhaps my expression told him more than my words, for he was good enough to look much pleased as he shook hands warmly.

Then we girls all came out together. None of us cared to hear the rest of the last number. I for one wanted to be quiet and think—or rather to hear again in my mind those haunting, exquisite strains. Is there anything in the world more marvellous than music or more indescribable than its hidden soul? And now I must to bed, and hear it all over again, I hope, in my dreams.

MÜNCHEN, *March 6.*

As soon as my greetings with Thuille were over to-day I hastened to congratulate him again on the success of his *Gugeline* music last Monday. This time my German was a little more fluent, and I even made bold to ask him how long it had taken him to write the act. He said that he started it in the middle of June, 1899. After waiting two weeks for text from Bierbaum, and after countless other interruptions, he finished it by the end of August.

Then began the lesson. With a sinking heart I placed my fugue on the rack. I don't know how many hours I had worked on it! At any rate the stretto had almost reduced me to tears. A stretto is a net, and if one is not constantly on the watch, he is caught in its meshes. Thuille looked it over, made some corrections, and to my surprise said, "*Sie sind recht fleissig gewesen, Fräulein. Die Fugue ist gut*" (You have been very industrious. The fugue is good). My spirits rose with a leap, for he seldom praises.

The pupil who was to follow me was late, so I had time as I drew on my gloves to express the wish that we might hear his new opera produced at the Hof-Theatre.

"I don't know about that," said he laughing. "I am fortunate if I have my *Lobetanz* given. I expect that will appear about the twenty-second of the month."

Turning, he opened one of the drawers of his desk. "Here are the complete scores of them all," he said, as he touched the backs of the great books with a tender, almost paternal pride; "and here is that place for the wood-wind in *Gugeline* which you remarked on."

He pointed out the passage in the score, and to my delight took his seat at the piano and played for some moments.

"The most laborious thing I ever did in my life was writing out the orchestral parts from here on," he said, playing the theme of the duet. "I thought I should never get it done."

His words made me think of something Mr. Chadwick had said in class one day, shortly after the completion of his lyric drama "Judith." He declared that reducing the orchestral parts so as to make a complete piano accompaniment was one of the most tedious things he ever experienced. After all, my dear, the gods are just, and to be great does not mean that one is free from drudgery.

Chadwick, by the bye, always had evidences of his energy on every hand in the form of proofs or manuscript lying carelessly about in his studio; perhaps a song, or a string quartette, or merely the key to his harmony book which he was getting out last spring. Thuille, on the contrary, has nothing to indicate what he is doing—except cigarettes.

After my lesson I stopped in at Polly's. I found her playing away at a fearful rate on Saint-Saëns' G minor concerto, and she looked so pale and tired that I made her call everything else off and go for a walk. We found, however, that by hurrying we could spend a half-hour in the old Pinakothek, and so we made our way to Barerstrasse. You must come over if only to see these splendid Holbeins! The master's portrait of himself is alone worth a trip, and then Dürer's four apostles! The St. Paul is my favorite, he is so majestic, but Polly prefers St. Mark. She says he looks happier than the others.

I must not forget to tell you about taking tea at the Sterners'. They live over by the river, and we wandered through a maze of streets before reaching the right house. Then we climbed numberless flights of stairs in true German fashion, and found ourselves in the most charming apartment under the very roof itself. Mrs. Sterner received us in a picturesque, low-studded room, which had at one end a large bay-window, where the tea table was spread. She is very slight and girlish in appearance. As we sat sipping our tea I continually caught tantalizing glimpses of a big studio at the farther side. It was not long before the artist himself entered and invited us, when we had quite finished, to see his "work shop."

Such a fascinating place as it is, not at all of the conventional order, with bizarre nick-nacks and curios, oriental hangings, and stale, tobacco-scented air; but a big, light-flooded, healthy room adorned merely with sketches, pictures and easels, for the Sterners have only pitched their tent in Munich for a brief season and are off in the spring for Italy.

There is a wealth of treasures in Mr. Sterner's portfolio, and his field of work is a delightfully broad one. Of his illustrations, those for a new edition of Edgar Allan Poe's works interested me most. Each picture had such definiteness about it that one could guess at once the lines it interpreted. Two of his most famous paintings which we asked to see were in America, but he showed us the exquisitely taken photographs. One represents a charming child, the other is that which I have seen so often in your own music room,— William Mason at the keyboard.

"And the new picture, is it finished yet?" asked Edith, who had been there before.

"It's the old story!" he said; "I've put it aside to work on pot-boilers!"

Fancy calling those wonderful illustrations of his by such a brutal name.

Thursday.

At last, my dear, I have something definite to tell you about Fräulein Hartmann. The most distressing thing occurred at dinner to-day. Just as we were having salad and composedly conversing about Arabic customs—a favorite subject of Herr Doktor and the Poet—in came the Italian ladies, with profuse apologies for their tardiness. They had been "doing" the Bavarian National Museum, and lingered too long over the ivory collection. One of them crossed to Fräulein Hartmann's place and handed her a letter.

"I met the postman on the stairs," she said, "and told him I would take any mail up, so he gave me this."

Fräulein thanked her for her kindness, then, glancing at the handwriting, suddenly flushed to the roots of her hair. A second later her aunt, who had been looking over her shoulder, snatched the letter from her hand. Frau Von Waldfel's face was crimson with anger and her black eyes snapped maliciously.

"I'll look after this, young lady," she said, thrusting the letter into her pocket. "A pretty pass when engaged girls receive love letters from other than their betrothed."

Her voice echoed harshly in the complete stillness of the room. Fräulein's face was a study—anger, mortification, and resentment at the insult thus publicly inflicted on her. She started as if to retort, then, recovering her self-possession, she folded her napkin with dignity, rose and left the room. Her head was proudly erect, but her blue eyes, usually so tranquil, were smouldering darkly.

Frau von Waldfel looked even more enraged than before, that her niece should dare to depart without her permission. Muttering to herself, she pushed back her plate with a sharp rattle of her knife and fork, and went out with a heavy step.

We were all speechless with astonishment. The opportune arrival of coffee served to relieve the tension, and the calm voice of the Poet's Wife was like oil on tempestuous waters, as she inquired whether coffee were a favorite drink of the American people. When the meal was over she drew me into the hall.

"When you are through with your lessons come and see me in my room," she said.

That afternoon she told me the following about Fräulein Hartmann. It seems that Fräulein's parents, who live in Mannheim, are poor people. Her aunt, however, is extremely rich. When, last spring, Fräulein came out of the convent, Frau von Waldfel sent for her to pay her a visit. She was very ambitious that her niece should make a brilliant match, for she is, as you must have guessed, an intensely proud woman. Indeed, so anxious was she that she offered to pay the dowry and introduce Fräulein into society. This offer was accepted with delight by the Hartmanns, and Fräulein made her début in Berlin, where her aunt had taken a fancy to spend the winter. Among other men whom she met was Lieutenant Blum. He had, without doubt, heard the rumors of Frau von Waldfel's wealth, for he immediately began to pay court. Matters were speedily arranged between the two families and the young people were betrothed. Fräulein's parents were greatly pleased; Frau von Waldfel, radiant. Such an honor that her niece should wed an officer! Only Fräulein Hartmann did not seem to rejoice as she should over the good fortune. She would have been less than human had not all these beautiful surroundings, these fascinating frocks and these flattering friends of her aunt pleased her. But there was another man—there always *is* a third person when you stop to think of it—in form of a student, who had lived next door to the Fräulein all her life. He loved her, and she was half in love with him. In fact, affairs would speedily have come to a climax had not Frau von Waldfel taken it into her head to send for her niece just as their love-affair was at this critical point.

"As time has passed," continued the Poet's Wife, "the less she has cared for the lieutenant and the more she realizes that her feeling for Heinrich is deeper than the passing fancy which her family would have her believe. Don't blame her, my dear. You American girls are brought up very differently from ours here, and it is hard for you to understand. The letter to-day was, I feel sure, from Heinrich. Much as she has longed to hear from him, she is too honorable to permit any correspondence. A short time ago, however, Heinrich wrote a letter without her aunt's knowledge, and begged her to see him. After much misgiving she consented and a meeting was arranged——"

"At a carnival ball?" I interrupted.

"Yes. How did you guess? Probably the rash fellow has dared to write and propose another scheme. 'Lovers and madmen have such seething brains,'" she quoted.

"How will it all come out, I wonder," said I, puzzled.

"Indeed, I am wondering the same thing. It was while you were in Meran, you know, that Fräulein told me this. Her aunt was ill with the gout, and one morning we went for a walk together. She was feeling very unhappy, for in some way an unpleasant rumor concerning Blum's past had reached her, and I suppose the dear child couldn't keep her heart pent up any longer."

At her mention of Meran my mind flew back to the day I had seen the man I thought was Blum on the Promenade.

"Was the lieutenant in town then?" I asked.

"No. He had been called away on some law business," she answered.

A caller came in just at this point, so we had no more opportunity to talk together. I feel perfectly sure now that it *was* Blum who was having such a gay time with that crowd of people. He may have used that law story merely as an excuse to take a holiday. I can't bear to think of that sensitive, lovable girl as his wife!

Dear me, Cecilia, this is a strange, strange world! One would imagine that with experience and the discretion which comes with years, things would straighten themselves out a bit; but the older one grows the queerer life is!

Yours problematically and abstractedly,

M.

VIII

March 22.

Cecilia dear:—

There is the smell of spring in the air to-day. As I passed through Odeons-Platz on my way to my lesson this morning the sun was flooding the whole square with a delicious warmth we have not felt for months. A soft breeze brought across from the Hof-Garten the odor of freshly upturned earth. In front of the Feldernhalle the pigeons were fluttering and whirling, now suddenly swooping down from the roof, then darting back again like arpeggios of light. Around the flag pole a crowd of laughing children were tossing crumbs, and then running shyly back into the arms of their bareheaded nurses as the birds flocked near. The scene, in a dim way, suggested the Piazza of San Marco, and I gave a sigh for a sight of Venice,— its blue, unruffled waters, its marble palaces, and the white dome of the Maria della Salute against its peerless sky.

That reminds me of a secret I have to tell you. What do you think? In April comes the spring vacation at the Conservatory, and *Mütterchen* is contemplating for us—mind you, I say contemplating—a trip to the Italian lakes. Think of it—Bellagio, Como, Lugano and all the rest! I don't dare give myself up to dreaming, however, for nothing about it is as yet definitely settled.

Frau von Waldfel and her niece have gone to Berlin. They intend to stay several weeks in order to complete Fräulein's already elaborate trousseau. My own opinion is, however, that the aunt has read Heinrich's letter and wants to get her niece away from Munich for fear she may meet him. Ever since that shocking occurrence in the dining-room neither Frau von Waldfel nor the Fräulein have come to the table, but have had all their meals served in their rooms. Of course we do not see the lieutenant now, for which I am duly grateful, but I do miss the Fräulein and our pleasant chats together.

The days and lessons have been going on just as usual save for the interruptions afforded by the celebration of the Prince Regent's birthday which came on the twelfth. Early in the morning Louise and Edith called for me to go to the great military mass at St. Michael's. It is a rare thing for women to have cards, for this service is held for the soldiers alone. According to directions we made our way up a flight of narrow stairs which led from the sacristy, and found ourselves in the corridor of a balcony. From this corridor lead several little rooms which are called by the theatrical name of boxes. Most of them are reserved for the royal family and persons of rank. The one which was allotted to us was almost behind the high altar and facing the entire congregation. We could not be seen because no light from the church itself fell on the little glass windows, tightly closed, which covered the front of our box, but we could see excellently, and I shall never forget the brilliancy of the scene. I could not help but contrast the sight before me with that which I had beheld within these same walls last Christmas Eve. Now the church was filled with a throng of men in dazzling uniforms—here a company of privates with white-plumed helmets, there a group of officers in the Bavarian blue and scarlet, in the farther corner a coterie of generals in cream-colored broadcloth, countless orders gleaming across their breasts. The members of the royal house were seated directly beneath us in the choir. They were in full uniform, and sat in great chairs of red velvet with kneeling cushions of the same color at their feet. On the altar steps stood a company of soldiers with black plumes to their helmets, while separating the men in the nave from those in the choir stretched a great orchestra.

What a wonderful sea of color it was! The sunshine pouring through the long windows made the gleaming swords, the shining helmets and the gold-fringed epaulets a thousand times more brilliant. At the close of the service the band suddenly struck up the Hallelujah chorus from the "Messiah." I cannot tell you how impressive it was to hear these familiar strains amid such strange surroundings. I thought of the many times I had heard them sung at home. Then as the trumpets rang gloriously out on that mighty phrase, "King of Kings!" and the whole orchestra came in *fortissimo* with the wonderful "Hallelujah!" which echoed and re-echoed in the lofty arches, a blur came before my eyes. Ah, Cecy dear, the world may call Handel old fashioned and laugh at his simplicity, but who has ever written a hymn of praise so powerful, so convincing as this?

On Monday, as usual, came the Weingartner concert. Beethoven's seventh was gloriously given! Weingartner takes the first movement slower than I have ever heard it at home, but in the *allegro con brio* he simply sweeps the orchestra along. At the close of the concert occurred the usual ovation, a number of enthusiastic admirers staying to cheer and applaud until the lights were put out. Weingartner's conducting of Beethoven without score is far more inspiring than any other directing I have ever seen, just as the words of an extemporaneous speaker are more forceful than one who confines himself to notes.

I was sorry that I could not go to the *première* of Thuille's *Lobetanz*, but I attended the second presentation and enjoyed it immensely. It is just such a dainty thing as one would expect from his pen but, by the bye, is not really an opera at all. The program announced it as a play by Otto Julius Bierbaum with music by Ludwig Thuille. At first, therefore, I was slightly disappointed, but the whole thing is so charming that I soon forgot my annoyance at the spoken dialogue. The Princess, whom Lobetanz loves, was beautifully played by Tordeck. In the second act there is a lovely bit, when Lobetanz (Herr Walther) plays his violin under the tree and sings of the Princess' eyes. The text is in reality a fairy tale, full of imagination and delicacy.

I was discussing the performance with the little Boer after my lesson at the school to-day when who should come breathlessly up the stairs but Edith. She had been to the house for me, and finding me gone had come down to the Conservatory.

"I want you to go shopping with me," she said. "Do come and help me buy a pair of shoes."

So we set out together towards Marien-Platz. Oh, my dear Cecilia, if you ever come to Germany, be sure and bring enough clothing of every description to last till your return. German ladies are not at all particular about the cut and fit of their gowns, and as for their footwear! Such a time as we had to-day trying to buy those walking boots! In the first place we could find nothing narrower than *d* and Edith has the daintiest little foot imaginable. Then all the shoes we saw were so broad, flat and shapeless, that they had a positively inhuman appearance. Edith said they looked as though they had been made for ducks. It was hopeless to try and make the Fräulein understand what was wrong.

"Of course it's—it's very er-serviceable," said I, holding a clumsy thing at arm's length and surveying it critically, "but isn't it just a little too broad?"

The Fräulein cast a withering glance at us. "Broad?" she said, "why it's not broad at all."

"Oh!" said I.

"And they suit perfectly the Countess von R——, Frau Excellenz von S———, Frau General-Secretariat M——."

"I'll go barefoot before I'll wear those boots," exclaimed Edith in English, her cheeks flushing, "and I don't care a fig what these ladies with the long titles wear!" Then, in German, "Fräulein, the shoes are quite impossible. Good morning."

With the bearing of an injured queen Edith swept out of the store, I following meekly, and the Fräulein gazing after us both in open-mouthed astonishment.

It was not till we were half way up the street that I dared to break the silence in which my companion had enveloped herself.

"It occurs to me in a vague sort of way," I began timidly, "that the Baroness mentioned that a new shoe store had been opened on Residenz-strasse. I think she said they kept American shoes."

Edith's face softened. "Then by all means let us go there," she said. "I'm afraid the barefoot idea would be rather uncomfortable in bad weather."

Never did the qualities of American shoes appear so attractive as when we saw them invitingly displayed in the window of the new shop. Edith was so delighted at finding something that would fit that she paid without a murmur the fabulous price demanded, and invited me to drink chocolate with her afterwards at the Hof-café.

But just take a word of warning, Cecilia, and don't get caught in any such predicament yourself!

MUNICH, *April 2.*

The softest zephyr whispering to a rose; the faint fragrance of a lily swaying on its stem; a fairy cobweb lying shimmering in the sun; this is Beethoven as played by Ysaye. Never shall I forget his playing, and never do I want to hear any one else play the G major sonata.

Frau Langenhan-Hirzel and Ysaye are giving a series of concerts consisting of Beethoven's sonatas for violin and piano. Polly and I "went Kategorie" last week. To "go Kategorie" means that we used our students' tickets, or *Kategorie-Karten*, and obtained admittance at a reduced price. We did not receive a seat, and indeed none were to be had, for as we entered the hall of the Bayerische Hof, every place was taken and crowds were standing in the aisles. Accordingly, we made our way to the balcony, for beneath the windows there runs a low, broad step which answers very well in place of a seat. When we arrived, however, we found that this, too, had been taken possession of by a crowd of students who were sitting closely together, their knees almost touching their chins, and most of them holding the score on their laps. We were at a loss what to do, for that we might be obliged to stand had never occurred to us.

"There must be a step or a window ledge somewhere," said Polly, looking vainly about. Suddenly I spied a table in the corner, and I threw her a meaning glance. Quick as a flash she understood and was too good a Bohemian to be troubled by conventionalities. A moment later we were gravely sitting on the table side by side, our feet not touching the floor, our eyes not seeing the stage, but our ears straining to catch every note of that wonderful music. Polly had brought her score. One of the players in the Kaim Saal orchestra comes to her weekly and they read together, so she is familiar with all the sonatas. But after a time I shut my eyes to the printed symbols. I wanted only to hear, for from the moment Ysaye draws his bow across the strings "the weariness, the fever, and the fret" fade away, and one lives in another world. I have never heard anything more exquisite than his *pianissimo*. So marvellously *legato* and delicate it is, like a thread of gold, that I held my breath for fear the tone might break. It reminded me of all that is beautiful and dainty and lovely. By some odd association of ideas, Shelley's lines about the lily of the valley came to me:

"The light of its tremulous bells is seen

Through their pavilions of tender green."

Frau Langenhan-Hirzel played delightfully. But what impressed me most forcibly about her and about Ysaye was their perfect control.

After all the word artist means nothing less than control. No matter how deeply an artist's feelings may be stirred, no matter how moved he may be by the intensity, the passion or the anguish of the moment, he must always be the master of his emotions. He must make others cry, weep, exult, but must himself, while sensing every suggestion, remain in perfect realization of the situation. Picture Elizabeth sobbing in the midst of the Tannhäuser prayer! Or Paderewski breaking off in the middle of a bar and burying his face in his hands! And yet an artist must feel more keenly than the average man. Verily, the gods demand miracles!

How happy I am to write you that the trip southward bids fair to be realized within a short time. We have heard from friends who have landed at Naples and who hope to meet us at Milan. You can imagine how delighted we are to think of seeing some one from home, for letters at best are unsatisfactory things. I have so many questions to ask about everything and everybody that I shall be worse than the proverbial small boy.

Mütterchen and I have been down to Promenade Platz this afternoon buying trunk straps. Every time we return from a trip we find that our straps have mysteriously disappeared and no one seems to know anything about them. I fancy that those solemn-looking guards could enlighten us considerably if they chose. The weather was so delightful that after we had finished our shopping, which had led us down Maximilian-strasse, we decided to take a stroll along the Gasteig Promenade by the Isar. We found ourselves in the midst of an idly sauntering throng, for the greater part of München had turned out to luxuriate in the sunshine. Oh! my dear, how it would shock your fastidious taste to see the new *Reform Kleid*. All winter the women showed unpleasant symptoms of adopting this form of dress, and now that spring has come the fever has burst forth. The garments are all entirely in one piece, hanging straight downward, without shape or curve, totally ignoring the existence of a waist line. Most of them suggest nothing so strongly as *robes de nuit*, and some which have straps over the shoulders remind one of a feminine species of overalls. They are invariably too short in front, and as the fashion for white shoes prevails (may the gods spare you the sight of white shoes on German feet!) the effect is grotesque in the extreme. I believe the one virtue of these remarkable gowns is that they are comfortable, but so are bathrobes, sweaters, and négligés.

Even such a disturbing element as the *Reform Kleid* was in time forgotten, for it is very lovely down here by the Isar, that same "Isar, rolling rapidly," of which everyone has read. In place of green banks are high walls of white stone over which trails picturesque ivy from the terraces on either side. The Promenade itself stretches along the edge of the embankment, under great shady trees. So delightful was it that we wandered down to the Peace Monument and lingered there till six o'clock. The sunset was not especially brilliant, but the clouds which remained hanging low in the fast-darkening sky were wonderful indeed. They shaded from a dusky violet to deep, rich purple, and their music was that of a Chopin prelude, not one of those tempest-tossed visions, but perhaps the tender, half-melancholy one in B flat.

There is to be a *Vortrags-Abend* to-morrow night which marks the end of the spring term at the Conservatory. Fräulein Mikorey, a pupil of Stavenhagen's, is to play a Beethoven concerto, a student named Sieben is to play the violin, and I am to sing. Wish me luck, *Liebchen*!

Evening.

Just a line before I go to sleep to tell you that everything went off beautifully at the concert to-night. In one way it was an awful experience—*awful*, dearest of friends, in its most literal sense. This was not on account of the hall, I assure you, although it looked marvellously great and high as one stepped out of the dressing-room; nor was it because of the imposing audience, nor the crowds of pupils, who stood with critical attention around the sides of the room. Each of these factors may have its individual influence in striking terror to the heart of the timid performer, but they are all as nothing, absolutely nothing, I say, in comparison with that austere, black-coated, solemn-visaged line of professors who occupy the front row. You cannot imagine anything more terrifying than to stand on the platform and look down on this human barricade which shuts one off, as it were, from all that is friendly and encouraging. Stavenhagen sat in the centre, with arms majestically folded. On either side were the two women teachers of the school, and then to right and left stretched that line of frigid stateliness. There was a certain horrible fascination about it all, for try as I would to look over into the audience or up at the balcony, I found my glance always nervously returning to some dignified head posed at a critical angle, or some pair of hands with finger tips pressed together in judicial attitude.

The moment after I made my very quaint, very German courtesy—a ceremony insisted on by the Frau Professor—I suddenly became terribly conscious of the fact that I was an American, that all these people before me were German, and that I was about to sing to them in Italian. If I had dared,

I should have smiled. It was as if Italian were a language of commerce, by means of which I was to make a communication to the audience. But, dear me! I forgot all about that and everything—yes, even the depressing effect of the front row—when once I got to singing. And when it was over I could have hugged the fellow who cried "*Bravo! Amerika! Amerika!*" What mattered it that it was only an unpretentious pupils' concert? I could not have felt any prouder if it had been my début in grand opera when Stavenhagen and Thuille congratulated me, and the latter said, in his kind way, "We must make that counterpoint run as easily from your pen as those tones from your lips."

When one studies singing merely for the love of it, it is all very well, but it would make your heart sick to see the number of American girls over here who are half-starving themselves in order to study for the grand opera stage. One sadly wonders how many of them will ever "arrive," but when an argument is raised or a doubt expressed as to their ultimate success, they immediately cite the case of Geraldine Farrar, the American who is at present singing leading rôles at the Berlin opera house. The brilliancy of her success blinds their eyes to hundreds of utter failures, to countless half-way successes and to the untold drudgery which lies along the road.

IX

GORDONE, LAKE GARDA, *April 10.*

Dear Cecilia:—

I am writing in the loveliest and most romantic of gardens. It lies on the very edge of Lake Garda. Indeed, only a wall separates this wealth of green from the blue waves which plash rhythmically against their stone barrier. Above me are the apple blossoms; on either side lie tangles of vine and roses. In the distance are the neat white paths leading to the hotel where we are staying. It is not quite so civilized here as farther up the slope, where the plants grow in decorous rows and carefully laid out designs, but I like it much better, and besides, I get the breeze—a soft, *legato* breeze—from the water, and a sight of the picturesque island—as yet nameless to me—just across.

We found our way to this charming spot by means of our old friend, the Brenner Pass. How changed it all was from three months ago! Then everything was covered with snow, and the trees bowed into crystal arches under the heavy weight of ice. Now the whole earth seems made new with the soft green of spring. As we rode along every now and then we caught sight of a fruit tree in full bloom: peach blossoms of misty pink making their bit of valley all aglow, apple blossoms lighting up the shadow of a threatening, black mountain, whose snow-tipped summit seemed in some strange way akin to the patch of white at its base.

We reached Bozen at seven o'clock, and to our chagrin could find no accommodation at the hotels. In vain we pleaded with the polite proprietors. At loss what to do we followed in the footsteps of a stupidly smiling *Dienstmann* who had seized our luggage at the station and who now assured us he knew of an excellent inn where we could find rooms. Putting our trust in the gods we turned into the courtyard of a quaint little inn called the *Goldene Taube*, and inquired of the smiling Hausfrau if we could have lodgings for the night. With repeated courtesies she replied that there was but one room left, but it was a wonderfully beautiful room if we cared to see it. We assured her that we would take it on the spot, and gratefully climbed three narrow flights of stairs without a murmur. Though extremely primitive, the house was neat and clean, but we involuntarily exchanged glances when the landlady threw open the door at the head of the last flight and bowed for us to pass into the room she had so flatteringly described. Such a cubby-hole of a place, with a sloping roof, no carpet and one diamond-paned window, from which, by stretching out my arm, I could touch the window of the opposite house! Did I say no carpet? Then I most humbly apologize, for before each bed was a blue fragment which, by a powerful stretch of the imagination might, I suppose, be called a rug. The floor creaked unmercifully every time we walked across it, and we were terribly afraid we should lose something between the cracks. *Mütterchen* was inclined to regard the situation tragically, but I was rather enjoying the whole experience, secretly congratulating myself on being in an attic chamber which might bear some resemblance to those in which the great composers slept, ate, toiled and created their immortal works.

We had a walk and a drive the following morning and found Bozen much like Meran; both have the same dingy *Lauben*, the frescoed houses, the narrow streets and picturesque shrines. Our drive to Gries was through a veritable garden, for the fruit trees were abloom on every side. In the afternoon we took the train to Riva, a train which ran over the narrowest track I ever saw, high up on the mountains.

Riva is a charming place at the head of the lake, and has a most wonderful new road cut through tunnels of rock along the precipices of the west bank. I bought four oranges just as we were going on board the boat for the ridiculous sum of twenty heller (five cents). You should have seen the man who was selling them. He looked like the genuine villain of comic opera. He wore a black, broad-brimmed hat pulled low over his eyes, a full cape, which fell to his feet, with a collar of well-worn fur, and gold earrings. He was very gray and wrinkled, and oh! how he tried to cheat me! I had not had the sad and bitter experiences of shopping in Rome six years ago for nothing, however, and so I determined to settle on a price and remain firm. Accordingly I offered twenty heller for four oranges. My Italian is not fluent. It is limited to musical terms and a few selections from grand opera. I tried to recall something fitting, but the only lines which came to me were those of an aria from *Semiramide*, which could hardly be said to fit the occasion. How grieved, how shocked he looked—the old rascal!—as he assured me that he could not permit his wonderful fruit to be so cruelly sacrificed, although nothing would delight him more than to please the American signorina. Accordingly I turned to go in dignified silence. In a second the oranges were done up in paper and given over, with the astounding announcement that never before in his life had he allowed his fruit to be sold at so absurd a sum, but—with a telling glance from under his black hat—the charms of the signorina were irresistible. At my first opportunity I told of the bargain I had made.

"Twenty heller for four oranges!" exclaimed the gentleman who sat next us. "Why, my dear young lady, for thirty heller (eight cents) I just bought a whole dozen!"

The sail down the lake is a beautiful one. Such picturesque little towns nestling down by the shore, such bewildering orange groves along the hillsides, such quaint spired churches perched in the most inaccessible places!

The "witchery of the soft blue sky" enchants one. The lake, too, is of a wonderful tint. What a land this must be for artists! Such color, color everywhere! I wonder they don't all come over here and live forever.

The card which I sent you from München, told you we were going straight to Milan, so you doubtless are wondering how we chanced to stop off here. Just as we were leaving Garda our boat ran aground. This caused the wildest commotion among the townspeople who came flocking down to the shore and stood in lines along the breakwater—the women and girls bareheaded, with red shawls about their shoulders and blue aprons over their short skirts, the men and boys in loose shirts, with scarlet handkerchiefs carelessly knotted about their throats and any sort of a cap on the back of their heads. They shouted to each other, they gesticulated wildly, they speculated on the length of time before we could be launched. Indeed, I do not believe there had been as much excitement in the little village for years. So long were we delayed that on inquiry we found that we should arrive too late to catch the train for Milan, and on the suggestion of an English lady with whom we had become acquainted in that delightfully informal way known to travellers, we decided to stay at Gordone over night. That is how I chanced to be writing in this fascinating garden and to be hearing how Italian birds sing their morning pæan.

I did not have time before leaving München to tell you of the last two concerts we heard there. The first was the presentation of Bach's St. Matthew under the direction of Zumpe, with the Hof-Theatre chorus, orchestra and soloists. It strikes me that the Germans do not know how to sing oratorio. They lack that broad, *cantabile* style. Indeed, this branch of music is heard least of all here. Outside of the Rhine towns, which, I hear, have occasional festivals, little interest is shown in oratorio. At the St. Matthew the artists sang unsympathetically, but the choral singing was magnificent. Is there anything in the world grander, more truly religious than a Bach choral? One listens and the complexities, the sordidness, the trivialities of life all vanish. One feels only his own insignificance and humbly raises his voice with the rest in adoration of that Greatness which is eternal.

The other concert was the last one in the Weingartner series. The hall was packed with people, many of whom were standing. The program began with Cherubini's overture to Anacreon. Then came a delightful concerto by Haydn for strings, two obligato violins and an obligato 'cello. Last of all was Beethoven's ninth symphony. The stage had been enlarged to accommodate the big chorus. This was the first time I had ever heard this stupendous work. The singers sang with great spirit and as though they loved every note. What a magnificent main theme that is with the rushing counterpoint in the strings! I should think the clarinet players would be in their element, there are so many lovely bits for that instrument. And the drum in the scherzo—who could ever forget it?

At the close of the concert Weingartner was presented with an enormous laurel wreath, amid the prolonged cheers and applause of the audience. After coming out repeatedly to bow his thanks, he finally expressed them in a graceful little speech. I was too far away to catch all that he said, but at the end his *Auf Wiedersehen bis nächstes Jahr* (Till we meet again next year) brought forth a tremendous thunder of applause. And so exit Weingartner. I do hope I shall see him conduct again before I leave Germany.

This afternoon we take the boat across the lake and then the train to Milan,—so *addio carissima*, as they say in this lovely country.

MILAN, *Easter Sunday*, 1.20 A. M.

Easter Sunday is just beginning, and I am about to retire after an evening spent at La Scala in hearing Verdi's *Un Ballo in Maschera*. Am I living in another world? Can Germany and the dear old Hof-Theatre be but a day's trip away? When one has for months been going to the opera at seven and returning at the discreet hour of nine-thirty it seems nothing less than wild dissipation to find the final curtain falling in the wee small hours o' the night. Milan and München may bear a certain euphonic similarity, but they are really as unlike as black and white.

In the Munich opera house we are generally directed to our seats by a languorous gesture of the hand and a pertinent glance towards the desired row. Here, however, the usher seized our checks, muttered to himself, shouted excitedly to a fellow-usher, tried to direct us and several other people at once, urged us to hurry, and finally landed us breathless in our places. There were yet five minutes before the overture.

La Scala is an enormous opera house, and its stage stretches beneath one like a great plain. To be sure, after a winter of Wagnerian harmonies, Verdi's music sounded somewhat colorless, but oh! the language! I cannot tell you what a peaceful, refreshing change it was to hear a soft *Cielo!* issue from the soprano's lips, instead of the *Ach, Gott!* to which we were accustomed; and to remark how easily the tenor floated along on broad *ahs* instead of struggling over a succession of gutturals. Don't imagine that I sneer at German. It is a grand, strong language, but for song there is nothing in the world like this melodious tongue of the South.

We were surprised and pleased to meet in the lobby Mr. P——, a Harvard man whom I had met at college. He is studying voice in Milan, and told me not a little about student life here. It seems that it is the height of a singer's ambition to make his début at La Scala which Toscanini, the conductor, rules with a rod of iron. The students receive no advantages in the way of tickets, as our *Kategorie-Karten* afford us in Munich. He also told me that opera monopolizes the field of music.

"It is true that Toscanini gives a series of orchestral concerts after the season, but they are, as a rule, unsuccessful," he said. "We have small chance to study purely orchestral music."

"Are many Wagner operas produced here?" I asked.

"Oh, yes, Wagner is growing in favor, but the Italians love best their own school."

The tenor, Zenatello, who sang Ricardo, seemed to be a great favorite. The audience applauded and cheered him repeatedly. Mr. P—— says he has been on the stage but a short time. There was one singer of whom the people decidedly disapproved, to judge by the hissing which greeted him every time he made his appearance. I really pitied him, although he did sing atrociously.

The curtain fell at twelve o'clock. To our surprise a ballet, or rather a pantomime followed. It was a most elaborate production lasting an hour, but had nothing to do with what went before, and to tell the truth I was too sleepy to enjoy it much. And now good night. We are off for the lakes on Monday.

X

MUNICH, *May 11.*

Cecilia dear:—

We have seen the lakes and are back in the *pension* once more. Although I intended to send you a line from there we have been so constantly on the go that letter-writing has been an impossibility. Of course we "did" Milan thoroughly. On Easter morning we heard mass at the glorious cathedral. The music, rendered by two boy choirs with organ accompaniment, was very fine. After it was over we climbed up on the roof. As I stood there among the myriads of fairy-like spires, carved columns and slender pinnacles, I realized for the first time the meaning of that oft-quoted phrase, "architecture is frozen music." It was as though a whole orchestra were playing *con sordini*.

We had a delightful trip to Pallanza, rowing across to Isola Bella, where Napoleon slept before the battle of Marengo, and on to Menaggio and mountain-girt Lugano; but of all the places I saw Bellagio remains in my memory as the most charming. I think *der liebe Gott* must have said to Himself, "Here I will make the loveliest spot in the world." I cannot begin to describe it to you, but will try to tell you about it when I return.

At our first dinner after we came back we were surprised to find Frau von Waldfel in her old place. We had expected she would remain much longer in Berlin. Fräulein's chair was, however, empty, and I learned that she was ill.

"She is overtired," explained her aunt; "but if she does not improve by to-morrow I shall call a physician."

During the entire meal she spoke much more gently than is her wont, and did not engage in a single discussion about her food. I really think she is anxious concerning Fräulein's health.

The time seems frightfully short as I look ahead and realize that in two months it will all be over. I wish, indeed, that the days were longer. I am working very hard just now; there is so much to accomplish by the end of June! After all, life is a grand opportunity to develop the possibilities in a person, and although the greater part of us who want to do something worth while will never attain our goal, I believe we are all the broader and better for the struggle. Heigho! The little brown bird on the tree outside squints up his eyes and says in very translatable German bird-talk, "Cease philosophizing, American stranger, and set to work on the thing which lies nearest." Therefore, good-by for the present, and a fresh attack on my fugue!

Tuesday evening.

The doctor came to see Fräulein Hartmann last week and has been here daily since. This morning he pronounced her illness pneumonia. Every one in the house from Georg and Gretchen to the Poet himself feels very anxious about her. A quiet, black-gowned sister of charity has been installed as nurse, and the farther end of the floor below transformed into a miniature hospital. Lieutenant Blum daily inquires after the patient. If he does not come himself he sends his orderly.

Yesterday as I chanced to look out of the window I noticed a young man seated on a bench under the trees looking intently up at the house. His glance seemed to be directed towards Fräulein Hartmann's window. A half-hour later I saw him walk slowly, thoughtfully away. It was the same man who was in the arbor at the carnival ball—and must be Heinrich. You may be sure that I shall keep you informed about the Fräulein, for she is very much in my thoughts at present.

The one break in my regular routine of study this week has been a visit to the clubhouse, or *Corpshaus*, as they say here, of the Suevia. *Mütterchen* and I were the guests of Herr Martens, who belongs to this student club. To my mind the most interesting thing about the house is that it was originally built by Ludwig II. for Richard Wagner.

We entered by a side door which led into a hall. On the right was a counter and above it, around it and beneath it, hung hundreds of beer steins decorated with the arms of the corps. On the left was a high rack full of pipes, beneath which were rows of short jackets trimmed with black, blue and white, the club colors. On a shelf was a pile of round black caps with bands of blue and white.

We passed through the low door into the hall or *Kneipe*. It is a handsome room decorated with flags, shields and foils. The furniture is dark and very richly carved. At the farther end the ceiling is dome-shaped and frescoed with the arms of the corps. Here the students meet evenings. The other rooms of the house are far less elaborate, and almost all contain pictures of students duelling, for in order to enter this exclusive club one must first of all be a good fighter.

The bowling-alley was a failure as a bowling-alley, but as a picture gallery it was a great success. Around the room ran a double row of students' photographs, about five inches in height. There were all sorts of students and they never failed to have the scarred side of their faces towards the camera. Each wore the cap of their corps.

"Now I must take you into the main house. This is only the ell, you know," said our guide.

"And—and do you fight there?" asked *Mütterchen* hesitatingly. I think she had visions of walking in on a crowd of masked creatures fiercely plunging at one another with swords.

Herr Martens laughed in hearty German fashion. "There is a small room up six flights in a house not far away," he said. "We hire it especially for fighting. You know that duelling of any sort is strictly prohibited by the police. But if one isn't a good fighter he cannot join the corps, so of course we have to have a place where we can fight secretly."

I glanced at his deeply scarred cheek and remarked that I had seen several students on the Parada Sunday wearing tightly fitting black skull-caps.

"That is because they have head injuries," he explained. Then he added proudly, "I have forty-two scars."

Mütterchen gasped. I endeavored to look properly impressed.

"But what *do* you find to fight about in these peaceful times?" I asked, after what I considered to be a reverential pause.

"Oh, anything serves as a pretext," he answered, quite frankly. "The students are always quarrelling over something or other. It's rather good fun to settle it by swords."

"And at home they call football brutal," murmured *Mütterchen* in my ear.

Making our way through reading-rooms, lounging-rooms and card-rooms, we came out on a delightful roof-garden.

"We sit out dances here when we have a ball," said Herr Martens.

Mütterchen and I both waxed enthusiastic, not only over the garden, but over the whole house, which compares very favorably with our handsomest college clubhouses in America. The only incongruous feature was the air-tight stove in every room. This fact brings forcibly to mind that in spite of everything else Germany is years and years behind us in comforts and conveniences.

I have been so busy lately that I have studied evenings too, so have heard but one opera since my return. That was "Louise," by the French composer Charpentier. It is distinctly modern and extremely interesting. Some of the scenes belong to the real *opéra comique*. There is one laid in a dressmaker's establishment. The curtain rises on a room full of girls sewing and gossiping. Suddenly a band is heard and the tramp of feet. You would have laughed to see the girls jump up on the tables and crane their necks to get a view of the soldiers out of the window! The finale is very effective and the whole thing has the merit of being essentially realistic. There is no coloratura soprano carolling gayly in the neighborhood of high C about her broken heart. There is no basso profundo singing a drinking song, and at the end descending diatonically till he lands on low D, solemnly assuring us there is nothing like

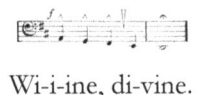

Wi-i-ine, di-vine.

nor any of the other traditional absurdities which we accept as a matter of course. On the other hand, it seems to me that realism carried to the *n*th degree is quite as ridiculous. In the fourth scene of the first act, Louise (charmingly sung by Morena) with her father and mother sit around a table in the centre of the stage for fully five minutes without uttering a syllable. What do you think they are doing? *Eating soup!* Meanwhile the orchestra is playing beautiful music, elaborating a theme which I called *motif du potage*. To what are we coming next?

Our table is not so deserted as you might imagine, in spite of the absence of Frau von Waldfel and her niece, for Fräulein Werner, the novelist, has come to stay some weeks at the *pension*. She is an odd-looking woman with shrewd brown eyes, red cheeks and very black hair. She talks a great deal and is decidedly interesting. You know that almost all her novels have been translated into English and are much read in America. She is, therefore, greatly interested in our country and asks many questions about it, although she declares that her fear of the sea will prevent her from ever setting foot on our shores.

Between you and me, I have generally found that people who "do things" are horrible bores socially. Nevertheless they have a certain charm, and that reminds me to tell you that I am to meet the opera singer Morena on Friday. Madame A——— is to give an informal tea for her and has asked me to come. You can fancy how delighted I am, for I can never forget her well-nigh perfect rendering of Leonora in *Fidelio* and her Elizabeth in *Tannhäuser*.

Sunday.

Such an enjoyable time as we had at Madame A———'s tea on Friday. We were entertained in the cosiest of roof-gardens, high up above the noise of the city. Morena did not arrive till late, but Bürger, one of the leading tenors at the opera house, was there with his pretty young bride. He it was who sang Siegmund in *Die Walküre*. At half-past five came the sound of laughter on the stairs, the sharp barking of a dog, and—enter Morena, dressed in a white gown with a big black picture hat. "What a glorious creature!" I said to myself. I have told you that she is very tall and handsome, with beautiful dark eyes. Her manner is utterly unaffected and charming. In five minutes she was laughing and chattering with us all, and consuming numerous chocolate cakes with all the enthusiasm of a child. Later it was my good fortune to have a talk with her all by myself in the course of which she asked many questions about America. She intends crossing within a short time, for it seems that Conried has heard her sing and wants to introduce her to New York audiences.

After she had gone—she stayed only half an hour—we all went into the music-room and heard a young American singer who has taken the stage name of de Zara[3] sing several selections from the rôles of Carmen and Santuzza. It was a great treat to hear her, for she has a voice of unusual promise. I wish you could have been with us! As a souvenir you shall see Morena's photograph which I shall bring back, with her autograph across the corner.

These are such busy days! We are finishing up the work at the school and rehearsing Berlioz's "Childhood of Christ" for the closing concert. This afternoon at my piano hour the little Boer girl didn't come, so I had double my usual time for reading at sight. Fräulein Fischer and I played the Saint-Saëns variations on a theme of Beethoven's for two pianos. Do you know it? I think it great, especially the big fugue at the end.

We have made two out-of-town trips lately, one to Starnberger-See and the other to the Isar-Thal. But it is time for me to go to my lesson now, so I shall have to save telling you about them till another time.

Believe me, dearest of friends,

As ever and always,—

M.

Fräulein Hartmann is about the same, and the doctor assures us that there is no immediate danger.

XI

June 28.

Confusion reigned on the floor below between the hours of four and five to-day—a somewhat muffled confusion, to be sure, for the proximity of the sick-room forbade any violent outburst, but none the less confusion of a most exciting character. As I came in from my composition lesson I found maids running this way and that, their arms full of clothing and packages. Georg and an unknown *Dienstmann* were carrying a trunk downstairs; Frau von Waldfel was kneeling before a hamper, giving orders through the open door of her room, while the Poet's Wife, a hat-box in one hand and a parrot cage in the other, was endeavoring to preserve order in the midst of chaos. She came out to speak to me as I halted on the landing.

"Frau von Waldfel has just received a telegram demanding her immediate presence in Budapest," she explained. "Some serious business complications have arisen, and she is hurrying to catch the six o'clock train to-night. Fräulein knows nothing of this and we do not dare excite her. Frau von Waldfel is greatly distressed at the thought of leaving her, and so I have offered to take charge of the sick-room during her absence."

"That is so like you," I said, impulsively. "I'll just leave my music books upstairs and come directly back, for perhaps I can be of some help."

When I returned Frau von Waldfel was standing in the hall, dressed for the journey. She looked anxious and preoccupied as she shook hands in a perfunctory manner and counted her bag, her bundle, her umbrellas and her parrot cage three times before allowing the servants to carry them down to the droschky waiting below. Then occurred something which makes me regard her in a far more kindly light than I have been wont to do. She took the hands of the Poet's Wife in both her own.

"What should I have done without you!" she said. I never dreamed that her voice could be so gentle. "Take care of the child and let me know daily how she is. Years ago I lost a little one of my own—the only child I ever had—and I couldn't bear to lose Minna too. Here, Georg," with a sudden change to her old peremptory manner, "take this bag down."

She turned to descend the stairs but there were tears, actually tears in her eyes, which softened their beady hardness and made them almost beautiful.

"Poor woman!" said the Poet's Wife softly, as we heard the rattle of departing wheels.

Then she hurried off to prepare the Fräulein's gruel, and I came up to write you. Really I do not know whom to pity most, Frau von Waldfel, the dear Fräulein, or Heinrich, who is eating his heart out from day to day.

Now to tell you of some of the things I have been doing lately. First, I heard *Die Meistersinger* for the second time. If one were to see a hundred productions of this wonderful work I am sure he would discover new beauties on the hundred and first hearing! Is there anything more lovely than the quintette? Is there anything more marvellously worked out than that street scene? Once I was so impressed by the complexity of the score that I actually forgot to listen and simply sat and wondered at the genius of Wagner. Feinhals was the Hans Sach, Fräulein Koboth, Eva, and Geis, Beckmesser. The opera began at six and was not over till after eleven, with pauses of fifteen minutes each between the acts. You would have laughed to see the bored expressions of two Americans who sat next us. They declared to each other, thinking doubtless that there was no one to understand them, that they never were so glad in their lives the final curtain fell. Why on earth didn't they rise and go out? Not two minutes later I saw them again in the *Garderobe*, and overheard the gentleman say to another American whom he had met, "*Delightful*, was it not?" while his wife joined in with, "Isn't Wagner simply delicious?" O departed gods of Olympus, is there anything more disheartening than this Fashionable Insincerity?

If my remarks about Fashionable Insincerity and Modern Indifference (for they are formidable enough to be capitalized) would seem to show a disbelief in the existence of that simple faith which the poet assures us is better than a long line of ancestors, believe me, appearances are misleading, for even if I had had a tendency in that direction the Corpus Christi celebrations would have banished it on the spot. These will always remain to me beautiful and sacred, and as an indisputable proof that Simplicity and Sincerity do not belong solely to a distant past.

On Corpus Christi morning we were called at six o'clock in order not to miss the great procession which for hundreds of years has annually on this day wended its way through the streets of the city. As we walked towards Max-Joseph-Platz we found everywhere the most charming decorations. Instead of conventional banners and bunting, rows of fresh green birch trees about six feet high were fastened against the houses as if growing up from the sidewalk. From the window ledges hung square pieces of cloth of red and blue. On turning into Theatiner-strasse what was our surprise to find a great altar erected in the very centre of the street. It was high and triangular in form, outlined by these same delicate birch trees. Yellow draperies of satin concealed the wooden framework itself. In the centre was a great crucifix, and the sight of this sacred symbol in the midst of a busy thoroughfare was startlingly impressive. Through the middle of the street, where the procession was to pass, grass had been strewn. But just as we reached the café the rain began to fall in torrents. This was the end of it for that day. The altar was hastily demolished, carts were driven up to carry away the draperies, and people with disappointed faces came crowding under cover. We learned that the procession must be postponed till Sunday, although the Prince Regent and the golden carriages—such an important feature of the occasion—would not appear.

Somewhat crestfallen, we returned to the *pension*. But by Sunday our interest had again awakened. This time it was not till eight o'clock that we stationed ourselves on a balcony overlooking the street, from which point we had an excellent view of the procession below. First came a number of priests in splendid robes, bearing a holy banner. Then followed a double row of little girls on each side of the street. Some of them could not have been over three years old. They were all dressed in white, with white wreaths on their heads, and carried bouquets of vari-colored blossoms. Between the two double rows were four little tots bearing the image of the Virgin. You have no idea what a lovely picture they made. Then came a brass band with a choir of bareheaded boys and students singing hymns. Behind were more priests with banners; a body of young girls in white, carrying unlighted tapers and chanting prayers in unison; sisters of charity, schoolgirls, then another band and a choir of older men, singing. Just below the house was one of these altars which I have described, built on the sidewalk against the side of a building. When the procession stopped for a few minutes a service was held here, several priests stepping out from their places in line to officiate. Those who were near turned towards the altar and followed the rites, while the others kept on with their praying and singing with intense devoutness and earnestness.

I wish I might describe to you how solemn and impressive it was—the voices of the chanting priests; the murmur of prayers rising from hundreds of lips; the distant music of those grand old chorals; the incense, floating up in thin clouds from the swinging censers below; above all the absolute simplicity and devotion of the people. My eyes filled with tears. Skepticism, doubt, hypocrisy, seemed to be merely delusions of another world. Unconsciously the lines of the Persian poet came to my mind, and I murmured softly to myself,

"He that tossed you down into the Field,

He knows about it all—*He* knows—HE knows!"

The school year at the Conservatory closes with examinations for which I am now preparing. Then as my last task Thuille desires that I write an overture. (A *finale* would seem more appropriate, wouldn't it?) My second theme came in a moment, but I wrote fully a dozen first themes before I found one which would answer my purpose. Now I am doing the most interesting part of all—the scoring for orchestra. Of course this is only for practice and I never expect to hear it played, but as Mr. Chadwick used to say, "The only way to learn how to compose is to compose," so good-by, while I go on with the development section.

XII

July 10.

Good news at last about Fräulein Hartmann! The crisis is past and she is much better. We all feel so relieved, especially the Poet's Wife, who is beginning to show the strain of the past weeks. Frau von Waldfel writes that her affairs are in a far worse condition than she anticipated. In fact she appears to be greatly disturbed, which accounts for her having written but twice since she went away. Lieutenant Blum called yesterday. He has been here but once since Frau von Waldfel's departure. Doesn't that strike you as rather extraordinary? I was in the room when he came, and I could but notice how closely he questioned the Poet's Wife about Frau von Waldfel's last letter. Indeed he seemed much more interested in her business troubles than in the condition of his *fiancée*. Is it possible that it is only her money that he is after? To tell the truth the thought has occurred to me before, but I never deemed it worthy of consideration till now.

Every day the Fräulein receives beautiful blue flowers such as one finds in the Isar-Thal if one looks carefully enough. The servants think they are the gift of her betrothed, so do not gossip over his nonappearance, but the Poet's Wife and I know better. We have not seen Heinrich daily pacing to and fro in the park opposite without learning many things. Do you know, when I see him looking up with yearning eyes at Fräulein's window, I always think of the poet in Bernard Shaw's "Candida." The expression of Heinrich's face says as plainly as words, "We hold our tongues. Does that stop the cry of the heart?—for it does cry: doesn't it? It must, if you have a heart."

Yesterday and to-day examinations were held at the Conservatory. At eight o'clock all the professors appeared in the dignity of frock coats and black ties. They shut themselves up in a large room on the top floor, and one by one the pupils were called in to be examined before them. The only examination which was really trying was that in the history of music. Had it been a written one I should have approached it with only the usual nervousness, but an oral test is quite a different thing when one is a foreigner. All the pupils filed in together and sat in a single row on the platform. Before us was the formidable mass of professors with folded arms. Just in front of them was Stavenhagen behind a table and two other men who wrote down what we said. Before the director was a box full of paper slips on which were written the questions. When a pupil's name was called, he went to the box, drew three questions, and declaimed his answers to the joint audience of pupils and teachers. As I have told you, whenever I am nervous my German becomes affected in a peculiar fashion. I find myself forgetting words with remarkable rapidity and I insist on employing the English order of expression, which, to a Münchener, is nothing less than a mild form of madness. However, I managed to get through by not allowing the amused faces of the onlookers to trouble me, and although I discovered afterwards that I had called "The Damnation of Faust" an oratorio and had mixed my genders in the most ludicrous fashion, I was successfully "passed."

Now only the concert remains before the school closes for the summer. Then we are to take our final trip before sailing for home. Our itinerary has been specially planned to include places of musical interest and we are to go to Mozart's birthplace, Salzburg; Leipsic, crowded with memories of Bach and Wagner; Vienna where Beethoven, Schubert, and Brahms lie buried; Berlin, Dresden, and Bremen. We may run down to Budapest, since we are so near, and thus have an opportunity to hear a *bona fide* Hungarian orchestra. Isn't that fine, and doesn't it make you long to be with us?

Now no more for the present, my dear, as I want my last lesson for Thuille to be a good one, and my orchestration work is unfinished.

July 17.

The blow has fallen! To-day the Fräulein received a letter from Frau von Waldfel, saying that she has lost everything, even her personal property, through an unwise investment. The poor woman is in great distress of mind with lawyers, creditors, and what not, but these lines at the end of her letter impressed me more strongly than all the rest: "I have just heard from Lieutenant Blum. He writes that he releases you from your betrothal, 'realizing that in this present trouble Fräulein Hartmann can have no heart for festivities.' The sly fellow has had private information of my affairs here, and doubtless learned that if I scrape together all I have there will be just enough for your dowry and no more. Evidently he had hopes of living on my income after you both were married. It seems as though my present ill-fortune were enough without enduring this fresh disappointment."

My cheeks burned with indignation as I read. "The English employ a word which just suits this officer of the German army, and that is *cad*!" said I, decisively.

Fräulein Hartmann looked at the blue flowers in her lap and smiled gently. There was a light in her eyes—a light indefinably beautiful—that I had never seen there before.

"Poor Auntie deserves all the sympathy you can give her," she said, "but as for myself—well, I haven't been as happy for months. I feel as though a great weight had been lifted from my heart. After all, *kleine Amerikanerin*," she continued naïvely, "don't you think that people are happier without a lot of money to look after? Although six months ago the thought of all the delightful things money could buy——"

"Including a lieutenant?" I interrupted, involuntarily.

"Yes, including a lieutenant," she smilingly went on, "dazzled me, and made me a bit contemptuous of my Mannheim surroundings, now I really believe that our little home there is the loveliest, dearest spot in the whole world."

"With Heinrich next door," I added.

"Perhaps nearer than next door," said the Poet's Wife, caressing the girl's blushing cheek, "at least if we are to believe what he told us this morning."

"Dear," said the Fräulein, taking my hand in hers and speaking in those sweet, earnest tones which made her so winning, "did you think me very wicked and deceitful that night at the carnival ball? It has troubled me so much—the thought that you must despise me——"

"I won't allow you to say that," I interposed hastily.

"Yes, it always is a despicable thing to do—to deceive," she continued; "but I did so want to talk to Heinrich, and explain to him how things were. He wrote me a pitiful letter, begging to see me just once, and I was so unhappy that I finally devised that meeting. Now that we have been through all this I feel sure that my parents will have no objections to our marrying. They have always been fond of Heinrich. It was only the thought of my brilliant match that made them ignore, as it were, his very existence."

"Just as soon as she is well enough to travel I am going to take her home," said the Poet's Wife to me. "Heinrich is waiting here in Munich to go down with us. He is doing very well, by the bye, in his law work."

"Yes, indeed," said Fräulein eagerly, "and sometimes next year when—when we are settled—you will come down and visit us—promise you will, *meine Amerikanerin*!"

I promised, and lingered a few moments longer to learn more of her plans. Then the Poet's Wife insisted that she had had excitement enough for one day, and we both left her leaning back in her chair and, with an expression of unutterable happiness, gazing dreamily out over the swaying tree-tops of the Platz.

At three o'clock I was at Ainmüller-strasse for my last lesson with Herr Professor. Did I tell you that some weeks ago I made a translation into English of the *Rosenlied* (Rose-song) by Anna Ritter? Thuille has written a three-part song for women's voices to these charming words and asked me if I would put them into English for him. To-day he gave me the first published copy and wrote across the bottom the following inscription:

"*Meiner lieben Schülerin; zur freundlichen Erinnerung.* L. Thuille." (To my dear pupil in friendly remembrance. L. Thuille.)

I had brought as my lesson the overture for orchestra on which I have been spending considerable time lately, and a little song which occurred to me the other day at Tutzing. Nothing pleases Thuille so much as a completed piece of work, so I had worked very hard to finish the overture in time; in fact, even sitting up late at night, which is against all rules. He was pleased with the result and declared the song to be the best thing of its kind that I have done this year, which made me very happy. I did not mind that my eyes were tired.

"Take a good rest, Fräulein," he said. "You must surely come back to us all next year. And here is a souvenir, so that you will not forget your old teacher when you are in far-away America."

The souvenir proved to be a photograph of himself, taken from the large oil painting which hangs in the salon. Beneath it he had written his name with some bars of music from *Gugeline*.

I thanked him repeatedly as we shook hands. Then I went down stairs with a vague regret in my heart as I realized that the year's work was over.

On Tuesday evening occurred the closing concert at the Conservatory. The stage was decorated with plants, and a marble bust of the Prince Regent occupied the place of honor. We sang the "Childhood of Christ," by Berlioz, which, as I wrote you, we have lately been rehearsing. At the close of the concert came the award of medals for special excellency in the work of the school. Do you not feel proud when I tell you that out of the ten medals presented two were captured by American girls? Miss Bartholomay from Buffalo, a pupil of Stavenhagen, received one. Among the German girls I was especially glad that Fräulein Marianne Brünner, of Vienna, was awarded a prize, for I like her playing better than that of any one else in the school. She is also a pupil of Stavenhagen, and has unusual temperament and a splendid touch.

Mütterchen was very proud when it was all over, and she found me in the dressing-room exchanging congratulations with a number of pupils. It was hard to say good-by to them all, for the association which study of any kind brings forms a certain bond not easy to break. The little Boer girl, who is to stay another year, is terribly homesick for South Africa, and wept heartrendingly as we parted. The German girls all wished me a "*Gute Reise*" (pleasant journey), and bade me not forget München when I was again on American soil; my Irish friend, who sits next me in the chorus, promised to write and keep me informed of all the doings in the school; Fräulein Fischer and Frau Bianci insisted that I come another year and study with them, and Stavenhagen shook hands heartily and wished me success.

And now all that remains is to pack our trunks and shake the dust of Munich from our feet. I hate to leave the quaint old city and these warm-hearted German people, for I have grown very fond of both during my stay. Then there is the Obelisk and the Fountain, not to mention the other friends we must leave behind us. Edith and Louise have already gone to Paris, and Polly is somewhere in the Hartz mountains taking a holiday before starting for Vienna, where she is to study with Lescheticsky. In a few days we shall be scattered like leaves before the wind, some this way and some that. The year has been very rich in experience and pleasure, but, believe me, I shall not be sorry when we spread our sails for the harbor of New York and say to these friendly shores, "*Auf wiedersehen.*"

www.ingramcontent.com/pod-product-compliance
Ingram Content Group UK Ltd.
Pitfield, Milton Keynes, MK11 3LW, UK
UKHW031337260325
456749UK00002B/360